Women and Money

A PRACTICAL GUIDE TO ESTATE PLANNING

By
Patricia M. Annino, Attorney at Law

This book is an updated version of Women and Money: A Practical Guide to Estate Planning, originally published in 2004. The law has changed significantly since the book was initially published. This updated version incorporates the changes in the law to date and provides additional material to educate and empower the reader.

This book is intended to provide accurate and authoritative information and is sold with the understanding that this book is a guide and a resource. The reader shall not rely on it for legal, accounting or financial advice. If legal advice or expert assistance is required the services of a competent professional should be sought.

ISBN-13: 978-1461042327
ISBN-10: 1461042321

Cover and book design by Melanie deForest melaniedeforestdesign.com

THIS BOOK IS DEDICATED TO MY PARENTS,

Donald J. Annino and Patricia A. Annino

Introduction

WOMEN IN THE UNITED STATES TODAY CONTROL 75 PERCENT OF THE TOTAL PERSONAL WEALTH, fill more than half the jobs and earn more than half the college degrees. They make up the fastest growing sector of new business owners, the fastest growing sector of the U.S. investor base and, for the first time in history, nearly half of all substantial investors – those with more than $100,000 of investable assets – are women.

The projected transfer of assets from the World War II generation to baby boomers will likely provide women with even more capital. Women stand to inherit trillions of dollars in the next decade.

Yet, most American women have not yet taken steps to put the legal mechanisms in place through estate planning that will protect their assets, their families and themselves.

This book is for you.

Women and Money, A Practical Guide to Estate Planning is an exhortation, a resource book, and a trusted companion for women embarking on the estate planning process. Written by a woman attorney who has been advising clients – men and women – on estate planning for more than two decades, this book simplifies the details of estate planning, explains its advantages for women with both large and small assets, and guides readers through the process.

In fact, all women today should have an estate plan.

Wealthy women need to understand the gift and estate tax consequences of disposing of their assets, who is in control of their husbands' wealth if he dies first, and who is in charge of the couple's combined wealth when both die.

Lower income women with children need to use estate planning to explore ways to create wealth through life insurance so that, if something happens to them, their children will be cared for and the mortgage on the house paid off.

Single women need to decide whom they want in charge of their medical and financial affairs if they lose the ability to handle those decisions themselves.

Married women need to be knowledgeable enough to participate jointly in the creation of a family plan that assures there will be enough to live on in the event of their or their husband's death. They must also be comfortable with the advisors placed in charge.

Divorced Women need estate planning to establish guardianship for their children, confirm their former husband's support obligations, and plan how money will be handled in the most beneficial way for their children.

Estate planning can help *women in second marriages* consider prenuptial and postnuptial agreements, make sure their ability to live in a second spouse's home after his death is discussed and understood, and clarify to all what assets will pass to the surviving spouse and what assets will pass to the children of the deceased spouse. It can help widows manage their financial affairs at disability and at death.

Single women with minor children need estate planning to name a guardian for their children and the children's property, figure out how that guardian is to be compensated, how the financial resources should be used, and what adjustments might have to be made to accommodate the guardian and the larger family.

Estate planning can help *women with children who have special needs* – autism, depression, schizophrenia - to make appropriate arrangements to handle the care and financial considerations, including understanding what governmental assistance programs exist.

Women with elderly parents should use estate planning to explore long term care insurance, how their parents will be taken care of, how their assets will be managed, and make sure their plans are up to date.

Estate planning is one of the most far-reaching endeavors a woman can undertake, since it will continue to affect those she cares about long after she no longer can, but it is also one of the most complicated.

The Author

Patricia M. Annino is a nationally recognized authority on estate planning and a partner in the Boston law firm of Prince Lobel Glovsky & Tye LLP where she chairs the Estate Planning and Probate Practice Group.

She has taught courses in the Bentley College Masters in Taxation Program on Estate and Gift Taxation and Estate Planning. She has conducted more than 120 seminars on the subject for public and private organizations, including IBM, Mellon Bank, Northeastern University, A.I.C.P.A., Boston Tax Institute, Harvard Business School, Smith College, John Hancock Life Insurance Company, Merrill Lynch, Bank of America, Foundation for Continuing Education, the American, Massachusetts, and Boston Bar Associations, and the Massachusetts Bankers Association.

Ms. Annino has received the highest (AV) rating from the Martindale-Hubbell Law Directory and has been repeatedly selected by her peers as one of the "Best Lawyers in America" (Trust and Estates). She has been voted a Massachusetts Super Lawyer and a Top 50 Massachusetts Female Super Lawyer by her peers and an independent Blue Ribbon Committee (published in Boston magazine and Super Lawyer Magazine). In 2007 her peers in the Boston Estate Planning Council voted her the "Estate Planner of the Year". She is a Fellow in the American College of Trust and Estates Counsel (ACTEC).

She is the author of several professional texts, including Estate Planning in Massachusetts, part of West Publishing Company's Massachusetts Practice Series, and Taxwise Planning for Aging, Ill, or Incapacitated Clients, published by the American Institute of Certified Public Accountants.

She is a graduate of Smith College, Suffolk University Law School and Boston University School of Law, where she earned a masters degree in taxation. She is the recipient of Newton Country Day School of the Sacred Heart Distinguished Alumnae Award and the Suffolk University School of Law Outstanding Alumni Achievement Award.

For updated information and to subscribe to Patricia's blog visit www.patriciaannino.com.

Table of Contents

PART ONE
Your Basic Strategies

CHAPTER ONE

Plan Your Estate!

"One dies only once, and it's for such a long time!"
–MOLIERE

At least once a month I get a call from someone who asks me to please, please do just this one favor: She is going on a plane trip two days from now and wants something in place in case the plane goes down. She will inevitably promise that, upon her return, she will pay the appropriate attention to putting her affairs in order, come back to my office and do it more seriously and accurately.

I have learned, over the years, that they rarely come back and properly put their affairs in order. The next time this client calls will probably be right before her next vacation.

The first time a new mother leaves her young child with another family member or babysitter, she leaves detailed, explicit instructions and many phone numbers: Feed my child this. Don't feed my child that. This is the doctor's number. If anything at all happens, please call me. These are the phone numbers where I can be reached.

Estate planning is a way to leave instructions and numbers for a lifetime, a way to make sure that if anything ever happens to you, the person you want to take care of your children will do so, the instructions you have left behind will determine the kind of care they will be given, and your financial affairs will be in order.

Traditionally, "estate planning" meant having a lawyer write a will that explained how you wanted your assets to be given away at your death and named the person you wanted to be in charge of making sure the will's provisions were carried out.

Estate planning is quite different today. It is no longer a plan just for when you die. It is a plan for living, a plan designed to cope with the myriad of things that could happen to you or your family during your lifetime. Because people are living much longer these days, the

3

prospects of you or a family member living with a disability or in a diminished mental state are growing concerns. Estate planning enables you to select who will take care of you and your assets while you are living.

Estate planning (through gifting or trusts) is also a way to reduce or eliminate the taxes your estate pays when you die. In other words, it is a plan designed to make sure that as many of your assets as possible are passed down to the people or institutions you want to receive them, and as few as possible go to the government.

Estate planning is also a way for your survivors to avoid the expense, delays, and hassle of having to go to court to handle the processing of your will. Thanks to changes in trust law over the last 30 years, "living trusts" are now accepted legally. This means you can establish your trust now and transfer your assets to it. This enables your survivors to avoid probate, access your assets easier, cheaper, quicker and without the involvement of a judge upon your death. It also enables you to access those assets if you need them before you die.

It may be easier to understand the difference all these provisions can make – or, conversely, the impact *not* taking such precautions can have on your loved ones. Let us look at a real life example. Sophia, a single 40-year-old with a high powered career came to me a few years ago. Her father, David, had just died suddenly of a heart attack at 62 and Sophia was understandably devastated. Her parents had divorced when she was very young and remained estranged. Sophia, however, was close to both of them and had become especially close to her father in recent years. Her father's girlfriend, Anna, had lived with him for the last five years, but they were not married. Her father, who had vowed never to consult a lawyer again after his difficult divorce proceedings, had left no will and no directions of any kind indicating either what his financial assets were or who should get them.

I explained that when you die without a will, state laws dictate who will receive your assets. As his only heir, Sophia had to petition the court to become the administrator of his estate. That would also give her legal standing to determine what his assets and debts were.

It took two years and a lot of money in legal fees for Sophia to settle her father's affairs.

Legalese Defined

Estate: Your taxable estate includes the total value of all property you own at your death. Your liabilities are deducted from the asset values. In most cases the value is fair market value. Your probate estate is not the same as your taxable estate. Your probate estate includes any asset that is in your name alone at your death; it does not include most assets that you own jointly with a right of survivorship with another, assets that are already titled in the name of your trust, assets such as a life insurance policy, or annuity or retirement planning asset that pass to beneficiaries by contract.

Along the way, she uncovered some aspects of his life she had not particularly wanted to know about – letters from girlfriends, money he had given Anna and loaned to friends that would never get paid back.

Anna had been hurt and angered that David had not made any provision for her, that the title to the condominium had been in his name alone - even though Anna had contributed equally to the monthly bills - and thus she had no legal standing to remain living there. Sophia had decided to let Anna live in the condo rent-free for one more year before putting it on the market, but she worried endlessly about what she should or should not do for Anna, not wanting to be either too generous or too cold-hearted.

Things could have been much worse. David could have had many, many children and therefore many, many potential heirs and a much more complicated distribution of assets. But, as it turned out, by not leaving a will or any instructions, David left pain and angst to his daughter and his girlfriend, ostensibly the two people he loved most. Anna thought she should have been David's prime beneficiary and therefore felt both betrayed and mad at herself for not making sure he had taken steps to plan his estate. Sophia received about $500,000 from his estate, but was left with the nagging feeling that she was receiving those assets by default rather than by her father's volition. She thought he loved her more than anyone else, but she would never feel sure that she was the only person he intended to have the assets.

And, of course, Anna and Sophia, who might have helped each other out emotionally in their time of mutual mourning, were estranged by the process.

The only positive result was that the experience convinced Sophia that she wanted to take the steps necessary to make sure her affairs were in order. Since she was not married but still not discounting the possibility, we put a structure in place that could be changed any time her circumstances changed. I explained to her that since her father was dead and because she had no children, her mother was Sophia's heir at law, but Sophia knew her father would not have wanted any of his assets to be left to her mother. She decided to execute a will and trust that left the assets that came to her from her father's estate to a scholarship fund in his name, and left all of her own assets to her mother. She intended to change this when she married or had children. (And five years later married, with children, Sophia came back and did a comprehensive estate plan).

Sophia thus became part of an extremely small sorority of American women who have taken steps to plan their estates. Women have come a long way toward greater equality in the past few decades, but even today estate planning is something men do more easily than women. Men are still in higher places in the corporate world, more accustomed to dealing with accountants and lawyers on a professional basis and more likely to be approached by them for estate planning.

Women, especially married women, just don't think it is their responsibility to put the family affairs in order. Rarely does a married woman call me without her husband's involvement. Once the ball gets rolling, the responsibility is sometimes delegated to the wife, but the initiation usually starts with the husband. And that is a shame, because women are still outliving men. Leaving the responsibility up to the husband can lead to dire consequences.

Ten years ago a man who owned a restaurant was planning to take a business trip. Concerned that the plane might crash, he went into the back room, handwrote an instruction to his father, asking him to take care of his wife as the father deemed fit, called in two waitresses to witness the paper, took the paper to a notary three days later, went on the trip, lived and never thought about estate planning again…even seven years later, when the man found out he had cancer.

When the restaurant owner died of cancer, the father presented the paper to the probate court as a will and asked that it be allowed. The father and his attorney took the position that the son had intended his father to have all of the assets. The father decided that he would pay the widow a monthly allowance which would end if she remarried or had a new boyfriend. The widow came to me to seek advice. We went to court, taking the position that the paper was not a valid will. The case successfully settled – many months later.

It may be psychologically easier to "prepare" for the worst when you are a perfectly healthy person embarking on a business trip than it is when you are a cancer patient hoping against hope that the next cure will work.

But even the healthy have problems preparing. An intelligent, caring client of mine went through the estate planning process, worked out the documents she wanted to execute, asked me to draft them, reviewed and approved them… and then carried an unsigned will in her briefcase for ten years. She somehow felt that signing the papers would bring about her death.

We are a hopeful culture. No one wants to plan for death. No one wants to plan for disability. That is contrary to human nature.

Not doing so, however, is financially naive.

And if we are hopeful, we are also an extremely pragmatic culture, pragmatic enough to understand that poor estate planning or no estate planning can obliterate the hard-earned results of a lifetime of good planning.

It is your responsibility to make sure that your affairs are in order, that you have enough money to live on if your husband dies, that your family pays the least amount of estate taxes possible, and that you have designated someone to be in charge of your assets and your children. In other words, you must put the same level of thought into what would happen when you die as you have put into growing your assets and caring for your family while you are alive.

Do you need an estate plan?
To find the answer to that question, ask yourself the following:

☐ Do you have a well thought out strategy to make sure that if you or the prime bread-winner in your home becomes disabled or incapacitated your assets will be invested, your bills will be paid and your health care needs met?

☐ Have you designated a guardian for your minor children? If not, do you think you would agree with who the state picks out you?

☐ Do you have sufficient assets to replace your husband's income if he predeceases you?

☐ If you and your spouse die before your children reach college age, do the children have sufficient assets to both support themselves and pay college tuition?

☐ Do you have significant debt?

☐ Do you have elderly parents you are or may eventually be caring for?

☐ Are you responsible for the physical or financial care of any family member?

☐ Are you in a second or third marriage?

☐ Do you know who the primary and secondary beneficiary of all life insurance policies and retirement planning assets are?

☐ Will your assets avoid probate?

☐ Do you have a child with special needs?

☐ Do you understand the provisions your husband's plan makes for you?

☐ Do you know who your husband's advisors are?

☐ Do you know who would execute your plan at your death?

☐ Do you know to what extent you are controlled by the legal documents already in place and how those restrictions will affect you? Have you read them yourself, or did you husband summarize them for you?

☐ Do you understand your estate plan?

☐ Have you met your husband's estate planning advisors? Do you like them?

☐ Do you have enough assets to live on if your husband dies today?

☐ Have you determined how your husband's business will be turned liquid if he dies?

A well thought out estate plan will handle all those issues for you and many more. This is a complicated world. When designing your estate plan you will need to understand the impact of the transfer tax structure (the gift, estate, and generation- skipping taxes), what the probate process entails, and the legal mechanisms you can choose to implement your goals. It is up to you to be as creative as you want to be. The more effort that goes into the estate plan, the more effective it is likely to be.

Your estate plan should accommodate your assets, whatever they are in any given year, and accomplish your broad goals, but not be so rigid that if you sell your house or change your residence, the plan no longer works.

Estate planning is a process – it should evolve and change as you, your family and your circumstances do, as you move from single to married to parenting to divorced to widowed to remarried to grandparenting, and so on. It is prudent to meet with your advisors every other year and review where you are, where the law is and what your documents say. It is that commitment to the process which insures that your family is provided for.

Putting off the estate planning process carries with it two major risks: the significant possibility that your assets will not pass as you see fit to your intended beneficiaries and that your assets will be reduced by unnecessary taxes and settlement costs.

Estate planning involves self awareness and psychology. It forces you to come to grips with your mortality and deal with the possibility of future disability or incapacity and ultimately predetermine how your affairs will continue after your death. Taking the time to prepare eases the burdens on the family members and friends who will execute your plan in what will be for them an emotional and perhaps, chaotic time. Even if getting started is very difficult for you, get on the path of putting your affairs in order now. Remember to take one step at a time.

Step One

The first part of the process is to set your goals and objectives. Some of the goals you may wish to consider are:

- Designating someone to make your medical care decisions if you are unable to do so yourself.
- Designating someone to handle your financial affairs if you are disabled or incapacitated.
- Deciding who will manage your estate: Executor and Trustee.
- Deciding who is to receive your assets at your death.
- Understanding the tax consequences of your estate plan.

- Reducing the estate taxes, probate and administrative expenses.
- Making sure there is sufficient liquidity to carry out your intentions.
- Selecting guardians for any minor children.
- Providing for the orderly transition of family-owned businesses.
- Efficiently implementing any charitable gifting.

Step Two

You must organize all your financial information. Your attorney will need to understand what your assets are and how they are titled.

You should begin by listing your assets and their approximate values. If you have recently prepared a financial statement for a bank, that would be a good starting place. Last year's income tax returns are also helpful. The lawyer may provide you with an estate planning questionnaire that should be completed in advance of a meeting.

It is very important to understand who owns each asset and what the transfer consequences of each asset are. If, for example, your brokerage account is in a joint name you must decide whether you want the account to pass to the surviving joint owner at your death.

You must also decide whether that joint owner can withdraw funds or make investment decisions without your approval or signature.

You will need to designate the primary and secondary beneficiaries of each annuity, life insurance policy, retirement planning asset, I.R.A, Keogh, and so on.

It is important to understand how each parcel of real estate is owned. Obtaining a copy of the deed for each property you own and bringing it to the attorney is a crucial step. Frequently the attorney will review the documentation you have gathered and point out that the way you think you own assets is not necessarily the way they are legally titled.

Along with a presentation of your assets you should also be prepared to discuss with your attorney what those assets are worth. For gift and estate tax purposes, an asset is valued at its fair market value. The Internal Revenue Code defines fair market value as the price at which an asset would change hands if both parties to the transaction are not related and not under compulsion to sell. In other words, the fair market value is what the item would sell for in the marketplace if there were no compelling reason to sell it today.

In most cases you are planning for an eventual disability or death. That means that the value used when you are beginning the plan will probably not be the value of that asset at your death. The goal is to give the lawyer enough information so that he, or she can put together a plan that, to a certain extent, takes the shifting values into account. It is up to you, once you embark on the process, to remain aware of significant changes in values. You should review the plan with your advisors every few years to make sure that the way it was originally intended to operate still makes sense.

It is not necessary, in most cases, to value your tangible personal property (clothing, jewelry, artwork, etc.), unless they are very valuable. If an individual item is worth $5,000 or more in the market place today, it should be discussed.

Of course, you have spent more than $5,000 on furniture and other items in your home, but if you tried to sell those items today, it is unlikely that they would bring close to their initial price in current dollars. Jewelry, artwork, antiques and heirlooms, on the other hand, are more likely to retain their value, or even increase in value. If you have scheduled some of your possessions on a property and casualty insurance rider, then you should bring that rider with you to the attorney's office.

With liquid assets, such as cash, money market accounts, bank accounts and brokerage accounts, it is important to give the attorney an estimate of the value. It is not critical that the value be precise.

Real estate is difficult to value. You should have an idea of what your home would sell for in the marketplace today. Your town's tax assessment or sales of comparable properties in your neighborhood may lend guidance to that value.

If you own a family business, or if you started a business with others, its value should also be taken into account in your planning.

See the Wealth Assessment Exhibit at the end of this book which provides sample work-sheets you may wish to complete as a beginning step to gathering your information. You may also download these forms at www.patriciaannino.com.

Step Three

Now it is time to put together your team of advisors. Typically this will include an attorney who specializes in estate planning, a financial planner, an accountant, and a life insurance professional.

The best reference to finding advisors is often a satisfied customer. A recommendation from a family member or friend, or the relative of someone who has recently died and felt the deceased's plan was well constructed and efficiently executed might be useful in finding a good lawyer.

Your other advisors – the accountant or life insurance professional - may also provide you with names and phone numbers. The selection of your estate planning attorney is as important as the selection of your primary care physician. You are looking for an attorney with whom you can develop a relationship, because this attorney is going to hear a great deal of personal information and may, in fact, end up knowing more about you than any other person in your life. Clients have told me about illegitimate children, adopted children, their spouses and/or children's drug and alcohol issues. They have discussed the stability of their marriages with me and confided fears of divorce. Your attorney must be both technically competent and equipped with a personality that is a good fit with yours. The ideal estate plan is ongoing. Having a will or trust established and then putting it to the side is not effective. It is not doing an estate plan.

Check to see if the attorney or law firm has a website and review it.

The cost of a plan varies from state to state and depends on the level of complexity. The cost should be discussed with the attorney at the first meeting. You have a right to know how you will be charged. Some attorneys will charge on an hourly basis, others on a flat fee. Some charge for the initial conference, others do not.

Those who do not charge for an initial consultation take the position that chemistry is an important component of the attorney/client relationship and that should be ascertained before embarking on the process. Those that do charge believe that, regardless of chemistry and regardless of whether or not the engagement proceeds to the next step, very important information is often given out at that initial conference, and they should be compensated for providing it.

You may have to pay an up front retainer. This will be some or the total fee. If you terminate the relationship you will receive bacl the unused part of your retainer. If the amount of the legal fee exceeds your budget do not use that as an excuse to put off your planning. Discuss a payment plan with the attorney, or consider charging your legal fees on a credit card.

Before you go to your initial appointment it is a good idea to be prepared. Do your homework and pull together an accurate financial snapshot, listing your assets, liabilities and income. Include whose name each asset is in –for example yours alone, joint with another, or in trust. Find the names of the primary and secondary designated beneficiary of each life insurance policy, retirement planning asset, and IRA. Pull together the full names and addresses of each of your family members and intended beneficiaries. Give some thought to your choice of fiduciaries. See the Wealth Assessment Exhibit which provides sample worksheets you may wish to complete and bring with you to the initial appointment. You may also download these forms at www.patriciaannino.com.

CHAPTER TWO

Avoid Taxes

"Death is the most convenient time to tax the rich."
–DAVID LLOYD GEORGE

AS OF DECEMBER 2010 THE CURRENT FEDERAL ESTATE TAX EXEMPTION (TECHNICALLY known as the **"applicable exclusion amount"**) is $5,000,000 for those decedents dying in 2011 and 2012. It is not clear what the exemption level will be for subsequent years.

That means that if you die today and your total estate is worth $5,000,000 or less, your heirs will not have to pay any **federal estate taxes** on it. That's a lot of money – so much, in fact, that people have a tendency to think they don't have to worry about paying estate taxes, that estate taxes only apply to the very wealthy.

With this new law, that is true for federal estate tax purposes. However many states in this country have state estate taxes with a much lower threshold. In many states the state estate tax exemption is only $1,000,000. In some states the rate at which assets exceed that exemption can reach a 16 bracket.

It is important to do the math. The truth is, you may be wealthier than you think. Your gross estate includes everything in the world you own – your home, your money market accounts, your bank accounts, your cars, your art collection, your jewelry, your retirement plan, your IRAs, your business and life insurance proceeds, *everything*. And when you add all that up, you may find yourself more interested than you could possibly have imagined in examining ways to help your survivors avoid paying estate taxes.

Transfer Taxes

Estate Taxes: The taxes themselves offer an additional incentive for avoidance: Once you reach the estate tax exemption estate taxes are very, very high. This is true even though you have paid income taxes on your earnings your entire life. Under the current law, once your federal estate reaches the $5,000,000 exemption your heirs will end up paying 35 percent in federal estate taxes. In addition, if you are domiciled in a state that has a state estate tax or if you own real estate in a state which has a state estate tax then your estate will also owe state estate taxes. In virtually every state that has a state estate tax, that exemption is considerably lower than the federal exemption and the state estate taxes can be significant.

Estate planners use a number of techniques to defer, reduce, or eliminate the estate tax burden.

The Unlimited Marital Deduction: Husbands and wives (if they are United States citizens) do not have to pay taxes on their spouse's estate. As a result, if you are married, the easiest way to avoid taxes is to leave everything to your spouse.

This does not eliminate the problem, however. It just postpones it, because the estate you inherit tax-free from your spouse will be taxed when you die. What is more, if a spouse already has assets that equal or exceed the federal applicable exclusion amount (which is currently $5,000,000), then leaving additional assets directly to that spouse may intensify the problem because it increases the size of the estate.

Even if your combined assets do not (and are not expected to exceed) the $5,000,000 federal estate tax threshold, there may be a state estate tax consequence. As an example if the Smiths have total assets of $3,000,000. If Mr. and Mrs. Smith die in a car accident at the same time, their assets go federal estate tax free to their heirs, since their total $3,000,000 is less than the $5,000,000 federal estate **tax exemption.**

If Mr. Smith lives in a state which has a $1,000,000 state estate tax exemption, has $2,000,000 in his name and he dies first, however, his tax exemption is wasted. Mrs. Smith does not have to pay taxes on the $2,000,000 she inherits from her husband (unlimited marital deduction), but she now has an estate of $3,000,000. If she lives in a state that has a $1,000,000 state estate tax exemption, the $2,000,000 excess will be subject to state estate taxes and could reach $320,000 (16 per cent of the dollar amount above the million dollar exemption). Circumstances may prevent her from planning to reduce her assets – she could have been in the car accident with her husband, outlived him by several months and never gained consciousness. If she outlives her husband and is competent it is also quite possible the problem will increase as during her lifetime those assets will appreciate.

What happens when she dies?

Trusts as the potential solution: Mr. Smith could have made a provision in his estate plan (by coordinating his will with a revocable trust) that, in a sense, preserved his exemption. The provision would have stipulated that at his death, instead of passing all his assets on to

Mrs. Smith, his assets (any amount of money *up* to his allowable state exemption) would go instead into a trust that had been set up for the benefit of Mrs. Smith (and perhaps the couple's children and grandchildren).

Since Mr. Smith's assets went into this type of a trust and did not go directly to Mrs. Smith, they will not be considered to be owned by Mrs. Smith when she dies, and therefore have been kept out of her estate for tax purposes. In most states, Mrs. Smith can be the trustee of that trust. She can still access that money if she needs it. She can receive all of the income generated by the trust and can receive principal from the trust for health, education, support or maintenance. In some states, such as New York, it is mandatory that a disinterested trustee serve. A disinterested trustee is typically not a beneficiary of the trust and has no legal obligation to support any trust beneficiary. If a disinterested trustee is appointed along with Mrs. Smith, the standard for distributing the principal to Mrs. Smith is even broader. Using this type of trust would allow both Mr. and Mrs. Smith to utilize their state estate tax exemptions and be able to pass a total of $2,000,000 (not $1,000,000 between them) to their heirs free of federal and state estate taxes. Another reason to establish this type of trust (or to keep it in place if it was established for you when the federal estate tax exemption was less than $5,000,000) is that the new estate tax law which includes the $5,000,000 exemption is only scheduled to be in place for those decedents dying in the years 2011 and 2012. If the law then reverts to prior law the exemption will dramatically decline and the estate taxes will be significant. Utilizing this type of trust, known as a bypass trust, will significantly reduce the estate taxes your heirs will have to pay.

For income tax purposes it is generally not a good idea to have a tax-deferred asset, such as a retirement plan or IRA account made payable to a trust as doing so would preclude the surviving spouse from "rolling over" that asset and deferring income taxes until she reaches the age at which she would have to mandatorily withdraw it.

Disclaimer Will: Married couples who want to preserve the option of shielding inherited income from estate taxes but want increased flexibility in the planning process can try a fairly new arrangement known as the "disclaimer will." In this scenario, most of the assets pass directly to the surviving spouse but the spouse can "disclaim" or turn down any of the assets, and have them pass instead to a trust for the benefit of the spouse and the couple's children. (The will specifies in advance where the disclaimed assets will go.) The surviving spouse has up to nine months after his or her partner's death to decide what to disclaim.

The advantage of this is it puts off the decision until a time when the surviving spouse has a clearer picture of what the federal tax exemption will be (under the current law it is scheduled to change after 2012) and what the family assets are, and can therefore adjust the amount he or she wishes to either keep outright or to put into a trust that will bypass estate taxes. To be a valid disclaimer the strict rules set forth in the Internal Revenue Code must be followed. One rule is that during the nine month time frame, the spouse cannot even use the assets she or he is contemplating disclaiming. That means the surviving spouse cannot use a dividend check if she is planning to disclaim stock.

The disclaimer will is especially helpful to a married couple who is on the cusp of the federal estate tax exemption threshold and is not sure how much their assets will appreciate in the years ahead, how much the surviving spouse will need to live on, and what the tax exemption will be at the time of death. It also provides protection in case the law changes after 2012 and the federal exemption drops back down – it gives the surviving spouse a "second look" to decide how much of the surviving spouse's assets should pass into a trust that will avoid estate tax.

In a community property state the disclaimer rules are more complicated. If you live in a community property state be sure to consult with an experienced estate planning attorney before relying on the disclaimer.

For those who find the choice of whether or not to disclaim too overwhelming, there is a special type of trust known as a **Clayton Q-TIP trust** which gives the power to an independent trustee to decide how much passes to the spouse and how much passes to a trust to shelter taxes.

Portability: Under the new federal gift and estate tax law, the $5,000,000 exemption is portable between spouses (although there are restrictions on the dollar amount that may be portable if the person has been married more than once.) That means that even if the first spouse to die does not establish or fund a trust his or her five million dollar exemption can be applied and used when the surviving spouse dies. It is not clear whether or not this portability provision will extend past the year 2012 and the exemption of the first spouse is not adjusted for inflation, so even if the portability provisions are extended past 2012, under the current law if there is any passage of time between the date of the death of the first spouse and the surviving spouse the $5,000,000 figure is locked in. In other words, if with inflation the value of the $5,000,000 at the death of the first spouse would have increased to an amount greater than $5,000,000 by the death of the second spouse portability does not shield that appreciation from taxation in the surviving spouse's estate. On the other hand, having that $5,000,000 fund a trust at the death of the first spouse would shelter that initial $5,000,000 and whatever it appreciates to by the surviving spouse's death from the surviving spouse's estate. In addition, as of now, no state allows portability of the state death tax exemption so although portability may benefit those with a federal estate tax it will not benefit those with a state estate tax.

Another tool to maximize wealth and minimize estate taxes is an **Irrevocable Life Insurance Trust,** an insurance policy on, for example, the life of the husband in which a trust is named as beneficiary and the trust collects the proceeds after the husband's death. Since neither the husband nor the wife "owns" the policy, it is not part of either's taxable estate. The "trustee" selected by the husband must follow the husband's instructions on how the money in the trust is spent. The husband could stipulate he wants it used to pay his estate taxes, for example, or that he wants it given outright to one or more beneficiaries, or that he wants the proceeds to be kept in trust and provide periodic income to the wife or children or any other loved ones without giving anyone the full amount.

Federal Gift Tax; Lifetime Gifting: Another way to lower the amount of your estate that is taxable at your death is to give some of it away while you are still alive. This is an option for both married couples and singles whose assets exceed the federal applicable exclusion amount amounts (which for the years 2011 and 2012 is $5,000,000 per person). If your net worth is less than this amount, and you are single, or less than the combined amounts and you are married, then you may wish to gift for other reasons, but gifting for federal estate tax purposes is not necessary. If you are living in a state that has a state estate tax and not a state gift tax (such as Massachusetts), then gifting during your lifetime may reduce any state estate taxes that are due.

A tax advantage to gifting is that any appreciation in the value of the asset between the date of the gift and the date of your death is also removed from your estate. An obvious disadvantage to gifting is that once the asset is given away it is no longer yours. You will have lost control of the property.

Just as there is a federal tax on estates over a certain value, so there is a federal tax for gifts. Just as there is an estate tax exemption, so there are "annual exclusion amounts" for gifts – sums that can be given away without paying a tax.

At the moment each person, at the moment has an **"annual exclusion amount"** of $13,000. (This amount will increase with inflation.) This means you can give away $13,000 a year to anyone you please – and as many people as you please – and it won't be considered a taxable gift. These gifts can be in cash, fractional ownership in real estate, stocks or just about any type of asset you own.

In addition, you can pay any person's tuition or medical expenses – as long as payment is made directly to the school or medical provider – and it won't be considered a taxable gift. In other words, a couple could pay their grandchild's college tuition and also give that grandchild $26,000 annually ($13,000 from each grandparent). This amount is adjusted for inflation and will increase slightly over time.

If a gift is made to the grandchild directly and she is under age, then her guardian would be in charge of it until she reaches the age of majority – which is 18 or 21, depending on the state the grandchild lives in. These gifts can also be made in trust form. Many do not want to make an outright gift to a child, for example, because they intend for the gift to be used for a specific purpose, such as future tuition. They prefer to make the gift to a trust for the grandchild's benefit. If they do so, however, and they want the money removed from their taxable estate, then the trust they set up must be irrevocable; The person who sets it up cannot change it or amend it during his or her lifetime. Once it is signed it cannot be changed by anyone – the client, the lawyer, the grandchild – no one.

In addition to paying medical expenses, tuition, and giving away gifts of $13,000 annually, federal tax laws permit each person to give away an additional cumulative total of $5,000,000 in his lifetime without having to pay a federal gift tax. These larger gifts can also be made outright or in trust form. The federal gift credit is unified with the estate tax- you can give away the $5,000,000 during your lifetime and not have to pay a gift tax. To the extent you do not give it away during your lifetime it is available to pass estate tax-free to your heirs at your death. That means that under the current law, at least for 2011 and 2012 most married couples have a combined cumulative total of $10,000,000 they can give away during their lifetime or at death.

It is important to remember that the proverb - the tax tail should not wag the dog. Once you make a gift it is gone, gone, gone. When it is in the recipient's hands it is subject to their creditors, their divorce and if they have young children it will affect the ability to receive financial aid. You should also consider what would happen if the person you give the asset to dies before you do – do you know where the asset is going and how much control do you want over its disposition. In other words, there are many consequences to gifting beyond the tax consequences and it is important to understand all of the risks before embarking on a gifting plan.

Generation-Skipping Transfer Tax: In addition to the federal gift tax and the federal estate tax there is also a federal generation skipping tax. The term "generation-skipping" is slightly misleading. It does not mean that you have to skip the generation below (being your children) as beneficiaries of your estate plan. It means that you skip the federal estate tax that will be due at your childrens' generation level. The concept is quite confusing. Enacted to make sure that all family property above a certain amount would be subject to a tax at least once in each generation, this tax minimizes the amount of assets that can be passed on tax free to generations below your children. Currently this exemption is $5,000,000.

If an asset is taxed by estate taxes at your death, and then again at the death of your children, then by the time the assets reach the grandchildren, a significant amount of the value of the original asset will be lost to estate taxes. That's why some wealthy families establish trusts (either during their lives or to be effective at the time of their deaths) to skip the tax their children's estates will have to pay. This type of trust is commonly known as a **"dynasty trust,"** and it stipulates that when the donors die, the generation-skipping tax exemption amount will not be distributed outright to their children, but will stay in trust for the duration of their children's lifetime and bypass tax in the children's estate. If the funds are distributed to the child during the child's lifetime they are assets of the child and will be then included in the child's taxable estate – it is only if they are retained in the trust for the child's lifetime that they skip estate taxation at the child's death.

That is where the **tax skip** happens. If the trust had instead been distributed to the child during his lifetime, then the assets in it would be part of that child's taxable estate. By keeping it in trust (which can be for the child's benefit during his or her lifetime) and not giving it to the child outright, that child is not considered to have owned it for federal tax purposes. It is therefore accessible to him during his lifetime, but will bypass estate tax at his death.

These trusts typically run 90 years. If the trust is established in certain states, it never has to end and can be perpetual. Any appreciation in the value in the assets between the time they are placed in the trust and when the trust ends bypasses estate tax in the children's estate.

Charitable giving: Do you want to participate in involuntary philanthropy – that is, pay estate taxes and let the government decide what to do with your donations? Or would you rather play an active role yourself in where that money goes? Making a gift to a charitable organization will enable you to help those causes you deem worthy, while at the same time reducing your taxable estate. *(See Chapter 14: Protect Your Charity" for information on how to make a charitable gift that qualifies for estate tax deduction).*

Gifts to Individuals and Income Tax Issues: You are not entitled to an income tax deduction for a gift to a person, and, in the same way, your gift is not considered "income" to the person you give it to.

When giving property rather than cash, however, each asset has what is known as an "income tax basis" – that is what the asset originally cost (plus, if the asset is real estate, any improvements that have been made to it). When an asset is sold, the owner of the asset will pay a capital gains tax based on the difference between the original cost of the asset and the current sale price.

Legalese Defined

Generation-skipping tax: A tax applied when assets are transferred to a recipient (outright or in trust) more than a single generation removed from the transferor. For example, when a grandmother transfers assets to a grandchild.

If an asset is given to someone during the donor's lifetime, then the recipient of the gift inherits the donor's income tax basis in the property, and when the recipient sells that property, his gain would be the same as the original owner's. In other words, if this year your mother gave you $20,000 in stock in Gillette that she had owned for a long time, your mother would not pay any gift taxes on the transfer of stock and you would not be responsible for paying any income taxes. However when, at a later point, you sell that stock, you will incur a capital gain that is equal to the difference between the price your mother bought it for, if she paid for it, or the value of the stock when she received it by inheritance or, if she received it by gift, then the income tax basis that was handed over to her and the price you have sold it for.

The rules are different when the gift is made at death. If, instead of gifting you the stock during her lifetime your mother had left it to you in her Will at her death, then the $20,000 would be included in her taxable estate (even if there is no tax then due). When that happens the income tax basis in the stock steps up to the fair market value *at the time of your mother's death*. When you later sell that stock, any gain will be based on the difference between its value at the time of your mother's death and the price you get for it.

In most cases this will significantly reduce the gain. For that reason, many people take care to select for gift-giving during their lives property with lower capital gain and save the property with the greatest capital gain for gifts upon their deaths. That is also why, for federal estate tax purposes gifting is not always tax-wise if the federal estate is under or close to the federal applicable exclusion amount (which at least for 2011 and 2012 is $5,000,000 per person).

Patricia's Tips

What if you don't have a clue about the cost basis of the asset you sold and without it you are unsure how to calculate your capital gain? One strategy (and not one I recommend) is to assume the basis is zero and report all of the gain. If the asset is one your purchased records may be available. Stockbrokers are required under law to keep the basis records for six years and some brokerage houses keep them for ten years. If you bought the stock longer ago than that, try to remember the year you purchased it. Your old income tax returns may show the year you first received dividend income. Some websites, such as www.Bigcharts.com provide historical stock quotes. If you received the asset by inheritance the income tax basis begins again when the person who left it to you died. Check the probate courts to review the inventory to determine what the value was at the date of death. If an estate tax return was filed contact the executor to determine what value was listed on it.

CHAPTER THREE

Make Choices

"When you have to make a choice and don't make it, that in itself is a choice."
–WILLIAM JAMES

MOST PEOPLE SEE ESTATE PLANNING AS A PLAN FOR DEATH. FEW REALIZE THE ESTATE planning decisions they make may have a big impact on their future quality of life.

If you reach a stage where you are unable to handle your affairs, who will?

Do you really want a court to appoint a person or a financial institution to act on your behalf? Court supervised guardianship proceedings take time, cost money, publicly reveal your assets and liabilities and make public the embarrassing task of demonstrating your disability or proving you are no longer mentally competent.

Wouldn't you rather make these decisions yourself and in advance?

A key component of estate planning is putting the legal mechanisms in place when you are healthy so that if you become disabled or incapacitated, the person you have chosen will have the legal authority to access your funds to pay for your care and make the medical decisions for you that you would make. By planning ahead you will be able to exert control over your life even if you reach a stage when you are physically or mentally unable to do so.

Durable Power of Attorney: *A Power of Attorney* is a legal document in which you give someone else - or several people, or an institution – the power to manage your day-to-day affairs; the power to sign checks, for example, to pay bills, to make bank deposits, find the medical services you need, sell property, and so on. You need not be incapacitated to do so. People working overseas for very long periods of time, for example, often give someone at home the Power of Attorney to handle their U.S. property while they are gone.

A *Durable* Power of Attorney is a legal document you sign now that gives someone else – or several people, or an institution – that power both now and if *and* when in the future

23

you become disabled or incapacitated. To be a *Durable* Power of Attorney the document must say specifically: "This power of attorney shall not be revoked by my disability or incapacity." The document can also provide a line of successors. You could designate your husband, for example, and specify that if he is unable to serve, then your two children will have a joint Power of Attorney. The document should be clear and specific as to what "inability to serve" of your attorney or agent acting under the power means: His death? His disability? His decision not to act? Merely being out of the country?

A Nondurable Power of Attorney is revoked at disability or incapacity. All Powers of Attorney – durable or non durable – are lifetime documents and are revoked at death.

Some states authorize what is known as a **"Springing Durable Power of Attorney,"** one that springs into existence in the event of disability or incapacity. A significant problem with Springing Durable Powers of Attorney, however, is that many of those documents specify that one or two physicians must certify your disability or incapacity. Because the level of disability or incapacity is often not completely clear, many physicians – especially doctors who have had a long and close relationship with you – may be reluctant to sign the document without the approval of a court. This, unfortunately, just pushes you back into the situation that designating a Power of Attorney is intended to eliminate: bureaucracy, the involvement of external forces, costs, and time delays.

To clients who tell me a Springing Durable Power of Attorney sounds like a good idea because they prefer to postpone issuing the Power of Attorney privilege until they need help, I respond: "If you do not trust someone enough to name that person as your agent and give him or her the power to make decisions for you while you are competent, why would you give him or her the power to do so when you are incompetent?"

Should you become disabled or incapacitated and be unable to handle your financial affairs *without* a Durable Power of Attorney, then a family member has the right to go to court and become your guardian or conservator. Court supervision comes along with the court appointment, however. Some find that restrictive, others protective. If you are unsure whom to trust or which document is a best for you, then having the actions of your selected guardian supervised by the surrogate's court in your jurisdiction may not be a bad idea. Under the laws in most states, you have the right to nominate in your durable power of attorney the person you would wish to handle your financial and/or health affairs if a court orders that someone must be appointed in that capacity. Taking charge of this yourself and putting in writing who you wish to be named as guardian or conservator if it came to that is particularly important if the person you would select to act in that capacity is not the person who is your "next of kin" and is not the person who would normally be the court's first choice to appoint. If, for example, you are not married but are living with your significant other, then nominating that person in the durable power of attorney to act as your guardian or conservator if the court requires one to be appointed is strong evidence of your intent and a judge will give significant weight to that decision.

Under the Durable Power of Attorney, if you name more than one person, you should also make clear whether each person has the authority to act by himself or herself, or whether all signatures are required. There are pros and cons to both choices. If you name two people as your agents and either one of them can act without the other's signature, then you are putting less of a burden on a single individual, and tasks can be accomplished more efficiently. (One person can do the banking and sign the checks, for example. The other can manage the property).

On the other hand, if each agent can act independently, your affairs may lack coordination and checks and balances as well: there will be no way to stop a dishonest agent from acting unilaterally or to prevent financial institutions from relying on that person's actions.

What powers are included in the Durable Power of Attorney? Whatever powers you choose to include. The document you craft enumerates the scope of authority the designated agent will have. You can give him or her broad, general power, such as the authority to do anything with your assets that you, yourself, can do (as though the agent were you) without asking anyone else's permission or the court's permission. This can include the authority to borrow, to buy, sell, transfer, and exchange assets or to gain access to your safety deposit box. It can include the authority to run your business, pay your bills, file your tax returns, make investment decisions, make gifts, contract services, and deal with insurance and retirement transfers.

On the other hand, the powers might be very specific. You can make clear you are only giving him or her the authority to handle the sale of your home, or to transfer any assets that are in your name to your living trust.

For couples who own their assets jointly, the Durable Power of Attorney can be a very useful document, because it provides accessibility to assets that would, under many state laws, become frozen if one partner were to become disabled or incapacitated. For many couples the two most significant assets are their home and their retirement plans, both of which might be frozen – if a Durable Power of Attorney has *not* been established - when one partner is disabled or incapacitated.

If, for example, you and your husband own your home jointly with a right of survivorship and he dies, the ownership of the home will pass to you without the need of court approval.

If, however, he becomes disabled and lives, in most states you will not have the authority to sell, mortgage or transfer that home. Being married and having a joint title to the house does not give you the authority to sign his name and transact that asset.

Another asset that will become inaccessible is his retirement plan. At his death, if you are the beneficiary, then under contract law it will be paid to you. But, in most states, if he becomes disabled or incapacitated, even though you are his spouse, you do not have the authority to make investment decisions, emergency withdrawals or roll the assets over. Only he has that authority, and when he loses the ability to act, absent a Durable Power of Attorney, his court appointed guardian (or conservator) - which might be you - will have that authority.

In first marriages it is very common to execute Durable Powers of Attorney with each partner naming the other as agent. Some then name their children as successor agents. In second marriages, however, the Durable Power of Attorney can be more problematic as the interests between one spouse and the adult children of the other spouse can compete. That is all the more reason to give very careful thought to all the potential ramifications involved in selecting an agent and in deciding what type of authority you want that agent to have. If you have executed a prenuptial agreement, that may simplify the decision.

A Durable Power of Attorney can be useful in other family situations, such as when siblings co-own a vacation home or when a member of the family is living in a different country and needs someone to act as his agent back home. It is also common for an elderly parent who is not incapacitated but is just tired of handling all his or her affairs to give the authority to one or more children.

Agent Restraints: Under what circumstances should the Durable Power of Attorney permit the agent to benefit himself? This is an issue that should be reviewed and carefully scrutinized as part of the planning. It is common for spouses to give each other the full authority to do whatever they want with assets and benefit themselves without question. It is also common for the benefit to the agent to be restricted. As an example, if your elderly parent designates only one child to act as agent, that child's ability to make gifts to himself may be restricted.

The Durable Power of Attorney is a useful document, but, even when carefully constructed, not a foolproof one. It is based on a principal/agent relationship which means that the authority to act is there, but the obligation to act may not be. If, for example, you are disabled and there is a dispute among your children over whether or not your home is to be sold, the agent has the authority to make that decision, but he or she is not obliged to make any decision whatsoever. He can choose not to act, and if there are no successors named in the document and no ability to appoint successors specified, that may present a problem. The Durable Power of Attorney – and any estate planning document for that matter - is only as good as the person who is in charge of it.

Revocation: Because the Durable Power of Attorney is such a potent document, care should be taken to specify under what conditions and through what procedure it may be revoked. For many legal documents one need only record the revocation with the registry of deeds. In order to take no chances, however, if you wish to revoke a Durable Power of Attorney, you should submit a copy of the revocation on file with every single financial institution you have assets with. That puts the financial institution on notice that the agent no longer has the authority to act.

In Escrow: Sometimes people ask the attorney to hold the Durable Power of Attorney in escrow and release it only if they become disabled or incapacitated. The named agent cannot act without a copy of the document. Not all attorneys will hold the document in escrow, but this does provide one more safeguard, since the attorney should call you before releasing the document, and if you asked the attorney to hold the document in escrow and release it only if you become disabled or incapacitated, then the attorney would investigate that condition prior to its release.

Health Care Power of Attorney: There are actually two types of Durable Power of Attorney documents, one that designates an agent to handle financial matters, and another that authorizes an agent to make decisions about medical treatment. With the health care document (also known as a **health care proxy**) – as with the financial document - the agent's responsibilities are specified ahead of time by you.

You can authorize someone to supervise your care if you are incapacitated, to consent to have you undergo or to withdraw you from certain types of treatment, to make hospital or nursing care arrangements, and employ or discharge caregivers. The document can authorize everything including minor and routine medical involvement. It can give the agent access to all your medical records. It can also empower the agent to make such major decisions as whether or not to terminate your life.

As they do with the financial Durable Power of Attorney, in the health care area couples usually designate each other to make medical care decisions and list their children as successor agents. For those clients without spouses or children (or who are looking for alternative possibilities) I stress that your health care agent must be someone you trust who shares your value system, who is willing to perform the task, and who has a clear understanding of what your preferences are.

It is prudent to update this document regularly and when you update it to make sure that the most recent contact information for those you have designated to make your health care decisions (including all telephone numbers and cell phone numbers) are current. If your health care proxy was executed prior to The Health Insurance Portability and Accountability Act of 1996 (known as HIPPA) then your document must be updated. Under HIPPA, if you do not expressly waive your right to privacy in writing, hospitals and physicians do not have the legal right to speak with your health care agent or to release medical information to that person.

Living Will: If one of your preferences is to die a natural death, you may want to draw up a living will to specify your intent. A living will is a declaration that, if there is no hope of recovery, you do not want to be kept alive by extraordinary medical treatment or put on life sustaining machinery. A living will gives your doctor permission to withhold or withdraw life support systems under certain conditions.

Not all states recognize the legal validity of the living will. Even if the state does not recognize it, though, it still may be an important document, as it is a roadmap – an indication of what you would want done if you were in a condition to tell medical authorities yourself.

About 20 years ago in Massachusetts – a state which, because of a strong Catholic presence does not recognize the legal validity of the living will - there was a landmark case concerning a firefighter who was put on life support. He was not conscious. His wife became his guardian and asked that his life be terminated. The Catholic Church insisted that her husband was Catholic and it was against the tenets of the Catholic Church to terminate life before its time. A major legal battle ensued. In the end, the judge decided not to terminate the fireman's life, because he could find no proof that the fireman would have wanted his life terminated. The judge stated that if there had been a living will in existence, even if it was not legally valid in Massachusetts, he would have felt more comfortable ruling that taking the fireman off life support was something the man would have wanted done. The United States Supreme Court has subsequently ruled that competent patients may refuse medical treatment and medical treatment can be withdrawn from incompetent persons if there is evidence that person would have refused the treatment.

Choosing Your Health Care Agent: This important person may have different titles in different states (such as "health care agent," "health proxy," "patient advocate," "attorney-in-fact," "health care representative," or "health surrogate"), but the responsibilities are the same. This is the person you have chosen to make medical treatment decisions for you if you are disabled or incapacitated and therefore unable to make such decisions for yourself.

Couples usually designate each other to make these medical care decisions and designate their children as successor agents. It is also good to designate both a health care agent and a successor agent (choice #1 and choice # 2), in case you need help at a time when the agent you've chosen is not available. Which of your children should you choose? And which friend or relative should you choose if you have no spouse and no children?

The official requirements for health care agents vary from state to state, but most states simply specify that the person must be an adult (over 18) and must be someone who does not work for your health care provider or for an adult care facility in which you are residing.

Evaluating Potential Health Care Agents (an exercise)

_____   _____

NAME OF PERSON UNDER CONSIDERATION   NAME OF PERSON UNDER CONSIDERATION AS SUCCESSOR AGENT

Scoring Criteria: (1 is lowest, 5 closest to perfect)
Basis for evaluation:

1) Religious beliefs: Since the concept of withholding artificial life supports runs contrary to the teachings of several religions – most notably the Catholic Church – it is helpful to find a health care agent who shares your religious beliefs and your position on right-to-die issues. **SCORE:**

2) Willingness to take on this task. **SCORE:**

3) Strength to act on your wishes and speak out on your behalf (even if faced with doctors, institutions, or family members who disagree). **SCORE:**

4) Communication: He/she is comfortable talking to you about sensitive issues and capable of listening to and absorbing what it is that you want. **SCORE:**

5) Separation: This is a person who can differentiate between his/her feelings and yours and be able to do what you want done. **SCORE:**

6) Proximity: This is someone who either lives close or could travel quickly to be there when needed. **SCORE:**

7) Availability: This person is likely to be accessible and capable of performing tasks well into the future. **SCORE:**

8) Personal Understanding: He/she knows you well enough to intuit what is important to you. **SCORE:**

9) Negotiation skills: He/she can mediate conflicts between family members, friends, and medical personnel. **SCORE:**

Rating Chart:
(45) You have found your health care advocate
(40-45) Strong Possibility
(30-40) Where is the weakness, and how important is that issue to you?
(Under 30) Try a new name in the consideration box

Figuring Out What You Want

(These questions are designed to help you know yourself and to form a basis for discussion with the person you choose to execute your health care power of attorney)

1) The Pleasures of Health: How essential are these capabilities to your happiness?
(Score: Vital, Important, Mildly Important, Not important)
- Walking
- Enjoying the outdoors
- Eating, tasting
- Drinking
- Reading
- Attending religious services
- Listening to Music
- Watching television
- Avoiding pain and discomfort
- Being with loved ones
- Touching
- Being self-sufficient

2) Fear Factors: What are your biggest concerns about the end of your life? _____
_____
_____
_____

3) Spirituality: How much of your comfort and support comes from religion? From personal prayer? From interaction with clergy? _____
_____
_____
_____

4) If you had the power to decide, what would the last day of your life be like? Where would you be? With whom? What would you be doing? What would your final words be? _____
_____
_____
_____

5) Assistance Preferences Worksheet: It is useful to discuss with your health care agent (and family members as well) the types of assistance you might want, should you need help…… and to revisit this issue from time to time, because your preferences could very well change.

Looking at each of the different scenarios spelled out below, think through what your preferences would be by asking yourself the following questions:

a) Would I still want to live at home?

b) Would I want caregivers hired to help me out in my home?

c) Would I want to be taken to a rehab or assisted living center?

d) Would I want family members to care for me?

e) Would I want to live with one of my children?

f) Would I want one of my children or a relative to live with me?

g) Would I want my health care agent to make these decisions for me?

h) Would my answers differ if my spouse were still living at home?

Scenarios

- If you were unable to drive a car ___
- If you were unable to climb stairs ___
- If physical problems prevented you from being able to dress yourself ___
- If you had to use a wheelchair because you were no longer able to walk ___
- If you were unable to leave your home ___
- If your vision were seriously impaired ___
- If your hearing were seriously impaired ___
- If you needed kidney dialysis ___
- If you needed chemotherapy ___
- If you were in physical discomfort most of the time ___
- If you could no longer control you bladder ___
- If you could no longer control your bowels ___
- If you could not think clearly ___

Long Term Care: Nursing care is very expensive today, as is home health care. And since nursing costs have been increasing by about five each year, arguing that you won't need that type of help for a long, long time does not mean you will be able to afford it if and when you do need it.

For that reason, many people look into long term care policies, which provide for custo-dial care when people are unable to perform what is known as **"the ADLs"** – the activities of daily living by themselves, like dressing, eating, bathing, or going to the bathroom.

Disability insurance will replace the income you lose if you're unable to work due to ac-cident or injury, but disability provides no coverage for long term care. Your health insurance - and Medicare – will pay your hospital bills and cover medical care for illnesses or injuries, like cancer, a broken leg, a stroke or heart attack, but these forms of insurance will also not cover help with the ADLs. A long term debilitating illness like Alzheimer's could deplete more than your own hard-earned assets. It could deplete your whole family's resources. In 2000 the average cost of an assisted living facility was about $25,000 a year. In 2010 the aver-age per person cost of living in a nursing home is $85,000 and by the year 2030 the average cost is projected to inflate to around $110,000.

Today, many couples are remarrying later in life and one spouse may have had a former spouse die after an extended illness. Many couples remarrying later in life want to be sure that their assets pass to their children, not to their spouse. When you marry you have a legal obligation to support your spouse – and that includes medical care. This obligation cannot be obviated by an agreement between the two of you or in a prenuptial agreement. If you are the wealthier spouse and you will be responsible for your new spouse's medical care you may want to consider purchasing long term care insurance for both of you to mitigate that risk.

There are nonfinancial reasons to seriously consider the purchase of a long term care policy. It is my experience that when a person or a couple has purchased a long term care insurance policy and a health disaster strikes, the person will receive care faster than if no long term care insurance policy had been purchased. There are two primary reasons for this. First, most long term care insurance policies include as a benefit- case management. That means there is an easy way to obtain the required care. The second reason is that when a parent has made an investment in a policy or when a family has made the decision that it is important to purchase that policy and care issues arise they are already acclimated and understand that it would be a waste of their investment not to activate the benefits under the policy.

There are many varieties of long term care policies on the market now, and the industry is constantly coming out with new products and new purchasing policies. Most require an annual payment from now until you need the care. The younger you are, the cheaper the policy, and once you buy one, you are protected from future medical issues that might pre-clude your insurability. Choosing a policy that provides for "at home care" is a particularly good idea, since everyone is more comfortable in home surroundings than in an institu-tion.

Writing An Ethical Will

You might consider writing an Ethical Will too. This is designed to enable you to pass **your values** on to your loved ones as well as **your valuables.** Writing an "Ethical Will" in addition to the conventional legal one that is the centerpiece of all estate planning can give you a chance to leave behind a spiritual legacy in addition to the material one. Ethical wills are also known as a "value" or "mission" statements.

Topics You Might Want To Include:

Values: You might discuss the **ethical** or **moral virtues** you have found to be most important in life, explaining how you learned them and why you are anxious to pass them on. You might share the role **religion** has played in your life; a prayer, a bible passage or religious music that is especially meaningful to you, memories of holidays, of attending religious services with your own parents or grandparents.

Life Lessons: What is the key to building a long and happy marriage? What are the advantages of enduring friendships? What is the best way to deal with difficult people? What have you learned from all those decades you put in on the job? Why have the philanthropic donations you have made over the years been important to you? How has motherhood changed your life? What are life's greatest pleasures? Life's most difficult challenges? Who were some of the most influential people in your life, people who shaped the person you are today? By looking into yourself and your experiences to come up with personal responses to such questions, you can pass on your acquired wisdom to later generations.

Family History: Who was the first of your ancestors to come to this country? Where did those ancestors come from? How did the family business get started? Who is who on the family tree? How did you meet your husband? When and why did you decide to buy the house your children grew up in? What is Aunt Helen's cheesecake recipe? Family details large and small might be lost forever if you do not record them for posterity.

Memories: Were there moments in history that affected you personally? Which are the anecdotes about your children (and grandchildren) that you cherish most, the moments you can describe to let them know how important they have been to you? Memories of your parents? Siblings? Of growing up in an era that people may not understand today?

Explanations: Why did you specify in your living will that if there was no hope of recovery you did not want to put on life sustaining machinery? Why did you decide to leave your youngest daughter the painting in the hall and your oldest son the silver set? Explaining such thought processes can prevent future in-family arguing.

Ethical Wills give you the chance to be remembered *the way you want* to be remembered.

[SUGGESTION: Two pointers in avoiding the most common pitfalls in Ethical Will writing: **1) Be subtle:** *It is all right to explain yourself – why you did what you did and what you learned from it. But you want to avoid trying to strong-arm your relatives into following the path you have taken, or, worse yet, scold those who have taken a different path.* **2) Keep it honest.** *Don't use your ethical will as a means of making yourself look better than you deserve to look. These are not public relations vehicles. Asking a friend to look over what you have written with a critical eye before you sign off on it might be helpful.]*

For additional resources on writing an ethical will visit **www.yourethicalwill.com.** You may also wish to have your memories recorded in visual form. See **www.Memoirs Production.com** and the wonderful work done by Iris Wagner and her team.

After Death Decisions Can Be Made Beforehand: Death is a reality of life. Discussing it openly with family members and other loved ones can provide a healthy outlet for relieving fears and anxieties.

Do you want to donate your organs and tissues? Medical technology has made successful organ and tissue transplants cheaper, easier, and safer. As a result, donated organs and tissues are in great demand, and tens of thousands of people are presently on waiting lists for them. Organs and tissues are used for research and study as well as for transplants.

If you want to donate your tissue or organs to medical science, you should state so in your advance directive (form follows) and also inform your health care proxy and your family, since even if you have signed an organ donor card, your family still has to sign a consent form at your death.

OTHER DECISIONS:

■ Do you want to be buried?
If so, where? _____

■ Do you want to be cremated?
If so, what should be done with your ashes? _____

■ Do you want a headstone?
If so, describe it _____

■ Do you want to plan your funeral?

A Funeral Plan

Location of Service:

_____

Clergy Member You Choose to Officiate:

_____

What other speakers would you like?

_____

Is there someone you would choose to sing at the service, play an instrument, or read from the Bible?

_____

If you own a cemetery plot, where is it?

_____

What newspapers do you want to carry your obituary?

_____

What aspects of your life do you want included in your obituary?

_____

Do you have a favorite flower?

_____

Do you have a charity you would prefer donations be made to in lieu of flowers?

_____

What hymns or music would you like to have played?

_____

What Bible portions do you want read?

_____

What favorite anecdotes or stories about your life would you like mentioned?

_____

Who should serve as pallbearers?

_____

What other details of the service are important to you?

_____

Do you want prepay for your funeral?

How to do it:
- You agree to pay the funeral home a specified amount of money for a specified service (including caskets, burial plots, etc).
- You can enter into an agreement with a funeral home, and the money will be held in the name of the funeral home as trustee for you.
- You can deposit the money in a bank passbook account for the benefit of the funeral home.

The Advantages of Pre-paying:
- You can choose what you want.
- Funeral costs are rising 2-5 percent a year. By pre-paying for your burial plot, casket, and planned ceremony now, you can lock into today's prices.
- You save your family the costs.
- You save your family unnecessary extra costs. (Family members, emotional in their grief, have a tendency to overspend when paying for funerals for their loved ones.)

Consumer Tips:
- Choose a licensed funeral director who has a good reputation and competitive prices.
- Have a family member sit in when arrangements are being made.
- Make sure everything you talk about is put in writing and get copies for you and for your family.
- Tell family members and friends where you are keeping your copy of your funeral plan.
- If your funds are being invested by the funeral home, make sure the funds are secured and check over time to make sure the investment is keeping pace with inflation.

CHAPTER FOUR

Create Wealth

"Logic and taxation are not always the best of friends."
-JAMES C. MCREYNOLDS

"DO I HAVE ENOUGH MONEY?" THAT'S THE FIRST QUESTION I AM ASKED BY EVERY WIDOW, recent divorcee and woman on the verge of retirement. In reality, however, it is far better to ask the money questions long before you are widowed, divorced, or ready to retire:

There are all kinds of models and computer simulations available today to provide an answer. With the help of computerized mathematical tools, for example, a financial planner can program in your current and projected financial needs, your investment portfolio, and hundreds or thousands of market-condition scenarios to determine whether your investments will last throughout your expected lifetime.

In the Monte Carlo simulation - one of the most popular – if your portfolio is run through 10,000 projected retirement scenarios and it shows it is sufficient 8,000 times, that means there is an 80 probability that your current portfolio will not run out of money. Then you must decide what your tolerance for risk is – how low the probability of running out of money must be in order to make you feel comfortable.

Will you have enough to live on if your husband dies? Let's say he died today and you are 50 years old and you need $10,000 a month to live on until you reach 85. Let's also forget any pension plan benefits you might get. Ditto for Social Security. Let's assume that you can earn 7percent on your investments (7percent net after tax is a very high number, by the way) and that you want your income to keep pace with an assumed inflation rate of 3percent. You would need to invest $2,363,990 to accomplish this goal. If you wanted to have the income stream last to age 95, instead of age 85, you would need $2,815,139.

How much would you need if your husband became permanently disabled? Sadly, you would need MORE than if he died, because in addition to your normal expenses there would be his medical bills and other costs associated with his disability. Group disability insurance might be available from his employer. Individual coverage is also available, and you should get three proposals from three unrelated agents before making a decision. Tell the agent you want to get quotes only from companies with a "Comdex" rating of at least 90.

How will your children be supported if something happens to you and your husband? Life insurance on your life or if you are married, on your life and your husband's life,, owned by a trust for the benefit of your children, is the best way to cover this need. Since the children will not need the money forever, just until they reach their early twenties, a much smaller investment amount is needed. In order to provide $5,000 a month for 15 years, using the same assumptions as above, you would need an investment of $698,690.

What happens to those child support payments if your divorced husband dies? A good divorce decree requires enough life insurance on your former husband to cover not only the alimony payments, but also the child support payments, should he die before his obligation is over. You should be the owner and beneficiary of this policy.

If your business partner dies will you lose the business? Yes, unless you have the ability to purchase the dead partner's share of the business from his or her estate. The bombproof answer to this problem is a properly drafted buy-sell agreement funded with insurance (discussed later in this chapter) - unless both partners have sufficient assets.

How can you make sure you will have enough to retire? The best advice is: by starting EARLY! Let's say you need the same $10,000 per month, adjusted for inflation, to age 95, we have been talking about. Let's also say you have zero saved for retirement and you are 40 years old and want to retire at 65. How much would you have to save for retirement each month between now and age 65? $5,619. Now let's say you are 50. You need to save $10,685 per month to be able to retire! So, start early and be consistent.

These are all issues the estate planning process should be able to help you answer, for just as estate planning is designed to **preserve your wealth** by helping you avoid taxes wherever possible, it is also designed to help you **create enough wealth** to keep you and your loved ones financially secure.

Wealth Evaluation

Before you can understand how much money you need, you must figure out how much you have. Thus, the first step in creating wealth is determining how much money you make and what the value is of the investments you have and how much you will need in the future. This involves:

1) Estimating the changes that may occur in your income over the years (What regular raises do you anticipate? Do you plan to work less while your children are young? Will that mean income cuts?)

2) Reviewing your investable assets (Do you have savings accounts? Certificates of deposit? Annuities? Stocks? Bonds? Mutual funds? Stock options and brokerage accounts?)

3) Totaling your liabilities (Do you have student loans to pay off? Home equity loans? Car loans? Mortgage payments? Credit card debt?)

4) Projecting your financial needs and wants on the horizon five, ten, fifteen, or twenty years down the road. Will you be buying a new house? Improving the old one? Spending more for child care? Paying private school or college tuition? Providing care for elderly parents?

You should also consider the amount of money you will be able to save each year and how much you can reasonably expect that to appreciate.

Wealth creation

- -

Since most of us have financial obligations – present and future – which are greater than our available assets, we need to create wealth in order provide for our loved ones in the event of our death, or for ourselves, in the event of the death or disability of a loved one.

That's where **life insurance** becomes an important component of estate planning. Life insurance can be used to make up for a lost income, help pay the costs associated with an accident, pay off the mortgage, cover college tuition and retirement expenses or even keep a small business running. Regardless of whether you are single, married, divorced or widowed, you should explore the wealth creation possibilities of life insurance.

If you are a single mother, for example, a life insurance policy can guarantee that if you die before your children are able to live on their own, they will have adequate financial support and not be a burden to the guardians you've chosen to continue to raise them.

You can even be creative about the benefits. Margaret, a single mother client of mine, wanted her sister, Betty and Betty's husband, Tim, to be the guardians of her children. Betty and Tim had two children of their own and a lifestyle that was comfortable, but not luxurious. To ease both the financial burden and the stress that adding two children to Betty's family would create, Margaret decided to bolster her estate with a life insurance policy and stipulated in her will that if she died while the children were young, the insurance money should be used for her children and her sister's children equally.

She wrote in a letter that she wanted the insurance money to pay for an annual vacation for the entire blended family– to Disney World, or some other place of the guardians' choosing - and for summer camp, music lessons, dance lessons or summer vacations for each of the four children.

Margaret's goal was to use the extra wealth created by the insurance money to unify the blended family and to enable life to continue on with a semblance of normalcy.

A life insurance policy can also build up your cash on a tax deferred basis. Cash value life insurance policies offer cash accounts as well as a death benefit. For income tax purposes that money is not taxed to you personally and continues to grow as long as it remains in the life insurance contract. It could create a solid cushion of funds for you to borrow against later if you needed it or to use to increase your income in retirement. In many states the cash account value of life insurance policies cannot be touched by your creditors.

If you are a divorced mother, the court may have ordered that either you or your husband maintain life insurance policies to pay alimony, child support and/or tuition. The purpose of the policy in a divorce agreement is to insure that if he is paying you alimony and/or child support and he dies *before* the date those payments are scheduled to end, the life insurance will compensate you for the lost future income.

In such cases it is important that you make sure every year that the policy is in force and the premiums are being paid. Dorothy, a 40 year old divorcee with two teenage children found out after her ex-husband died suddenly that he had been having financial trouble and had stopped making premium payments on his life insurance policy. Because the life insurance payments had been court ordered, Dorothy was awarded a $500,000 judgment against her ex-husband's estate.... only to then find herself just one of many creditors vying for a piece of very limited financial resources. She ultimately recouped pennies on the dollars she was owed.

To make sure your ex-husband is maintaining his insurance policy, you might want to mandate in your divorce agreement that the policies be held in a trust and that the premiums be paid by an independent trustee, someone who is impartial and will have a fiduciary duty to make sure that the premiums are collected and paid on an annual basis, subject to a court order. The formal trust document would designate successive trustees who would step up to the plate and make sure the premiums are paid if the initial trustee resigns, dies, becomes disabled or is unable to continue to serve. You might also request that duplicate statements of premium payments be sent to your home.

If you are a divorced mother and you predecease your ex-husband, his obligation to maintain any policy for alimony purposes will, in all likelihood, end. So will his obligation to keep paying child support, since he will probably become the children's guardian and thus be responsible for paying for their care. The court order will cease.

That does not necessarily mean the children will receive adequate financial support, however. In many divorce cases the husband remarries, starts a new family, and has trouble dividing his resources among two sets of offspring. And if he is forced to choose between the children he had with his former wife and those he has with his present wife, the former wife's children might not fare well. Taking out life insurance may be the most foolproof way to insure that in the event of your death, your children will be able to afford to do all the things you want them to do, like attend college.

If you are married, life insurance can provide a way of compensating for the loss of either your income or your husband's at his death. This will enable the surviving family members to maintain the same living standard… but only if you buy enough life insurance. Over the years I've encountered many couples who are so awed by the total pay off of a life insurance policy they do not do the math to figure out what the annual returns may be. A $500,000 or even $1,000,000 life insurance policy sounds like a lot of money – and it certainly is a lot to come into the household income tax free. But if you take that $500,000 and invest it, on average it will generate $25,000 a year in income (5percent). Even the $1,000,000 life insurance policy will generate only about $50,000 a year in annual income. If, for example, your husband earns $75,000 a year, you need to choose a life insurance policy that will yield you the same amount of annual income.

Life insurance is also a helpful security measure **if you have a business partnership,** and are worried about what will happen to the business if something happens to either you or your partner. In most businesses, neither partner wants the other's family involved in the business, but at the same time each partner wants to be sure that if she died, her family would be provided for. This dilemma can be solved by a buyout agreement, backed up by life insurance policies. These policies (through the ownership and designation of beneficiaries) will specify that if either partner dies, the surviving partner is obligated to collect the life insurance and use it to pay the family of the deceased for the deceased partner's share of the business.

Another way to use life insurance to help sustain a business in the event of one partner's death is to take out a smaller policy on each partner's life that would be owned by and payable to the company. This could be used to provide emergency cash and fund a salary for a temporary replacement of the deceased partner.

Life Insurance Alternatives

There are many different types of life insurance in the marketplace today. **Term life insurance,** the lowest priced variety, covers you for a specified period of time and has only one function: to pay a specific amount to the designated beneficiary upon the insured person's death. Other types of life insurance, including **whole life, universal life and variable universal life,** have higher premiums because they provide a death benefit regardless of how long you live. Variable life insurance policies offer flexible premium payments and the potential to grow your cash, along with your death benefits, if the underlying investment options perform favorably.

Many women only need to create wealth to cope with the financial emergencies caused by a spousal death during those years when their assets are small but their earnings are growing. This is when their immediate and projected monetary needs are greatest – the children are being supported, the house is not paid off, the business is at a crucial stage of growth, or tuition payments loom. The goal, therefore, is to put enough insurance in place *during those crucial years* so that if, heaven forbid, something happens, the life insurance proceeds will compensate for the lost earnings and augment the survivors' financial base.

The best way to do so is by buying a **level term life insurance policy** for the number of years you think you will need it (5 years, 10 years, 20 years, and so on). "Level" means that your insurance premiums will never change. "Term" means the policy lasts for a specified amount of time. The shorter the term of the policy, the cheaper the policy.

If you buy a ten year level term policy, for example, the cost of that policy will stay the same for ten years, thereby enabling you to know how to budget the cost of the insurance. The premium for a 20 year policy is much higher because the insurance company is on the hook for twice as long.

For example, if you expect to pay off your mortgage within the next ten years, you may only want to cover that portion of your income that is paying down that mortgage with a policy that will have level payments that you will stop paying for at the end of the tenth year.

If you expect to receive a significant inheritance and your parents are in their 80s, you may only want to purchase life insurance to bridge the financial need between today and when you expect to receive your inheritance.

If, on the other hand, you can clearly see that, although your specific needs will change (paying off the mortgage, educating the children, reduced retirement income) during your lifetime, your survivors or you yourself will *always* have a permanent need for a lump sum of cash, then you may very well decide that a certain dollar amount of the insurance should be permanent.

Some Choices

Say, for example, you are 32 years old, married to a man of 35. You have two children, aged 3 and 5. Your husband earns $75,000. You earn $20,000, working only part time. You intend to work at a reduced level until the children are older. You own a $350,000 home with a $300,000 mortgage. Your current investable assets are $20,000. You are funding your retirement plans and are putting aside $10,000 a year. Neither of you expect to receive a significant inheritance.

Choice 1

You decide to purchase a $2,000,000, 20 year level term life insurance policy on your husband's life and a $500,000 twenty year level term life insurance policy on your life. Assuming you are both in good health, the annual cost of his policy (depending, of course on which company you choose) will be in the $950-$1,300 range and the annual cost of the policy on your life will be in the $380-$420 range.

You assume that your mortgage will be paid off if both of you live the 20 years. You intend to drop these policies at the 20 year mark because you expect the assets you are setting aside will appreciate and you do not anticipate that you will need these funds when your children are educated.

Should your husband predecease you before the mortgage is paid off, your first goal should be to pay off the mortgage from the life insurance proceeds and invest the remaining $1,700,000. You project that will generate $85,000 a year in income. That is slightly more that what your husband was earning and with the mortgage paid off you feel that is a comfortable income to live on.

You are not sure if you can pay for the children's' tuition with this dollar amount, but this is the most you want to spend on life insurance at this stage. The $500,000 on your life is intended to cover the cost of child care if you predecease your husband. It should generate $25,000 a year in income. Should you predecease him, the family will lose your annual $20,000 income, and the cost of day care/child care will increase. You know this is not a perfect solution, but feel placing the total of $2,500,000 of life insurance in place will put the family in adequate shape should disaster strike.

Choice 2

You decide to buy the same amount of life insurance as in the above example, but instead of buying your husband a $2,000,000 twenty year level term life insurance policy, you purchase a $1,000,000 twenty year level term policy and a $1,000,000 thirty year level term policy on his life because you feel more comfortable knowing that the second million could stay in effect at a fixed price for an additional ten years.

Assuming he is in good health, the average annual cost today for a $1,000,000 thirty year level term policy on his life is $1,030-$1,300. In 20 years you will have the choice of deciding whether to drop both policies, or to continue to pay for the second $1,000,000 for some part or all of the additional ten years.

It is important to note that if, at the 20 year mark, you and your husband had only gone with the $1,000,000 of insurance initially and then decided to purchase an additional $1,000,000 life insurance policy, your husband would then be 55 years old, not 35, may have had health problems, and even if he were still in good health, the cost of purchasing a new 10 year level term policy at that age would cost almost twice as much.

Choice 3

When you review the quotes among the range of choices you find that 30 year level term policies are only slightly more expensive than 20 year level term policies at your age. Your research also reveals that there is only a marginal difference in the annual premium cost for a $1,000,000 policy on your life, over a $500,000 policy as the pricing break point for the insurance companies is $1,000,000. You decide that it is cost effective to cover the cost of a 30 year level term for your husband and $1,000,000 for you.

Choice 4

You decide that part of your insurance needs will be permanent, and you know that if you intend to keep some life insurance in effect for the duration, the cost will continue to inflate as you age and your medical risks increase.

You decide that $500,000 is a comfortable coverage level that you will always have for insurance. You decide to buy a whole life insurance policy in that amount and the difference in level term. Whole life insurance provides permanent protection while building a cash value account. As your cash value component increases, you set the option to either receive dividends from the policy or apply them to the cost of your future premium payments.

Whole life insurance also gives you the option of borrowing against your cash value during the course of the policy, or cashing it in and receiving part of your investment back. The cost of this $500,000 whole life insurance policy on your husband's life is roughly $5,635 for about twelve years under what is called the "premium offset" method.

You may decide to purchase a whole life policy in that amount, not because it's the best investment but rather because it will provide you a cushion of cash value over time. In the event of an emergency you can tap this cash value with a loan or by surrendering the policy.

Choice 5

You might consider the "guaranteed universal life" option in which the premium and the death benefit are guaranteed forever. The premium for that would be about $3,358 each year for the rest of your life. The balance of the life insurance in your portfolio would be the 30 year level term or combinations discussed above.

Changing Needs

Once you put your insurance plan in place, do not consider it set in concrete. It needs to grow and change with you and be evaluated on an ongoing basis as your life, the tax laws and your family change. It is interesting that twice in the past few years I have seen the industry wide cost of life insurance come down – even though the applicant is older. This is because the life insurance industry readjusts its pricing periodically based on actuarial evidence of life expectancy. Combine this with the fact that the life insurance industry is very competitive, forcing them to bring new, improved and more cost effective products to the marketplace.

The cost of purchasing life insurance increases as you age and as you develop health issues. Policies cost more, after all, as life expectancy shortens. Nonetheless, many people in their 40s, 50s and 60s buy life insurance policies to create wealth. They just pay more than they would to purchase a similar policy at a younger age.

In selecting a life insurance agent you should first ask your advisors, estate planning attorney, accountant and financial planner whom they would recommend for someone with your issues. Friends or family members who are in situations similar to yours are also a good source for references. What you want is a knowledgeable life insurance agent who will take the time to understand what your specific needs are, be willing to explain to all the products that are available and their comparative advantages and disadvantages.

You also want someone who believes in customer service and plans to be there for you over the years to make sure the insurance program you are presently putting in place continues to be the right one for you and your family. If you are given several names of life insurance agents, find out which companies they represent and make sure those companies are highly rated.

You may also want to ask the agent his or her designated background in this field. Some of those designations are listed below. If you are not comfortable with the agents that you are meeting keep meeting others until you find one that you can create a long term relationship with. Sources to utilize to find a qualified life insurance professional include:

Chartered Life Underwriter (CLU)

Contact Information:
The American College
270 S. Bryn Mawr Avenue
Bryn Mawr, PA 19010
Phone: 1-888-AMERCOL (263-7265)
Fax: 610-526-1465
Web site: www.amercoll.edu

Life Underwriter Training Council Fellow (LUTCF)

Contact Information:
The American College
270 S. Bryn Mawr Avenue

Bryn Mawr, PA 19010
Phone: 1-877-655-LUTC (5882)
Fax: 610-526-1170
Web site: www.amercoll.edu

Chartered Financial Consultant (ChFC)

Contact Information:
The American College
270 S. Bryn Mawr Avenue
Bryn Mawr, PA 19010
Phone: 1-888-AMERCOL (263-7265)
Fax: 610-526-1465
Web site: www.amercoll.edu

Certified Financial Planner (CFP)

Contact Information:
Certified Financial Planner Board of Standards, Inc.
1670 Broadway, Suite 600
Denver, CO 80202-4809
Phone: 303-830-7500
Fax: 303-860-7388
Web site: www.cfp.net

Member of the Registry of Financial Planning Practitioners

Contact Information:
The Financial Planning Association
5775 Glenridge Drive, NE, Suite B-300
Atlanta, GA 30328-5364
Phone: 800-322-4237
Fax: 404-845-3660
Web site: www.fpanet.org

National Association of Securities Dealers, Inc.

1735 K. Street NW
Washington, DC 20006-1506
202-728-8000
www.nasd.com

Tips and Pitfalls

■ Your employer's group life insurance plan is not designed to fill your wealth creation needs. Such life insurance policies usually lapse as soon as you cease employment with the company. At that stage you may have health issues or be uninsurable. You should use the employer paid group life insurance as a supplement to your life insurance program, but not as a building block component.

■ Buy life insurance, if possible, that has a "convertibility option" – an option that allows you to convert from term to more permanent coverage without undergoing another physical examination. Under a convertibility option you will pay the rate for your then-current age, but if you have health issues, the company cannot charge you extra.

■ Be careful to properly fill out who the primary and designated beneficiary of your life insurance is. In most instances, where the insurance is intended to create wealth, the spouse should be the primary beneficiary. If your children are young, you may wish to name a trust for their benefit as the secondary designated beneficiary.

■ Life insurance does not have to be validated in a court of law if the beneficiary designations are properly filled out. If the beneficiary designation is incomplete or blank the proceeds may be paid to your probate estate and will become part of your assets that are subject to direct court supervision. Unnecessarily incurring probate hinders your beneficiary's immediate access to the funds and will unnecessarily make the proceeds subject to the general creditors of your estate.

■ Find a qualified life insurance professional you trust to work with. The goal is to create a relationship that will grow with you and your needs.

■ On the down side, the payment of life insurance premiums is not deductible from your income taxes. On the upside, the proceeds will be paid to your beneficiaries income-tax free. If the wealth you are creating is significant and would kick your net worth into a taxable estate situation, then neither you nor your spouse should own the life insurance on your lives. Instead it should be owned by and payable to an irrevocable insurance trust. (See Chapter Two for a more detailed discussion of what that entails.)

■ If you do not have sufficient cash flow to handle the annual life insurance premiums, consider asking other family members, such as your parents or in-laws to help you out. They are entitled to give each of you an annual gift and not have that gift count as a taxable gift. Paying the premium to assist you in protecting your family's financial future may be something they would consider.

■ Make sure that the life insurance company you purchase the life insurance from is highly rated. It is prudent to buy life insurance from a company that is rated AAA or higher.

PART TWO

Focusing on You

CHAPTER FIVE

Single Woman

*"When I was young I thought that money was the most important thing in life;
now that I am old I know that it is."*
–OSCAR WILDE

IF YOU HAVE NO CLOSE HEIRS, TO WHOM DO YOU LEAVE YOUR ESTATE? HOW CAN YOU
make sure you will have enough assets to pay for your nursing care if and when you need it?

There are many estate planning issues for single women, but the first priority should be
to protect yourself against the unforeseeable: to designate a person or an institution to handle
all your affairs if you suddenly lose the capacity to do so. Regardless of your age, it is vitally
important that you have the mechanisms in place to determine who will take care of you,
who will make medical decisions for you, who will manage your money, and who will write
out the checks if, for some reason, you become unable to do so yourself.

These are disturbing decisions to have to make, and sometimes when a decision is disturbing to reach we do nothing, either because we don't know what to do or because we
fear doing the wrong thing. In estate planning, however, if you do not make these decisions
they will be made for you by a court.

All estate planning documents are only as good as the person or institution you have
designated to be in charge – the person acting as your health care agent, your attorney under
your durable power of attorney, or the trustee of any trust you have established. Selecting
someone to play these roles ahead of time is vastly superior to having someone come forward in a crisis situation and gain control over your affairs, especially since, under such circumstances; the person who does come forward may not be someone you would choose.

What you are looking for. You need someone who understands your outlook on life,
is good at making medical decisions, and likely to choose health options for you that you
would choose for yourself, if you were capable of doing so. You need someone who is savvy,

reliable, and trustworthy in financial situations. You need someone who is practical, and lives near you.

If you are lucky enough to have one person who fits all those categories, you must also think about whom to designate as that person's back up – in case he or she dies or becomes disabled or has circumstances in life that make it difficult to act on your behalf.

The advantage of designating a group. All those characteristics may be difficult to find in one human being, however, especially since this very responsible person probably already has a full life. Dropping your life on him or her is not exactly doing this person a favor. For that reason many people select either a major financial institution or a family member or friend backed up by a major financial institution, or a team of individuals acting together. This way the responsibilities can be divided, and if something happens to one of the designees, then others can substitute.

Estate planning issues for single women vary according to age and stage of life. The following case studies illustrate some of the variables.

Case Study 1: Emily, 32 years old, single.

Emily, a 32 year old working professional in Manhattan, making a good salary but not having much in the way of assets, wondered if she needed to have a will or any other kind of legal documentation.

I explained to her that at this juncture the only assets she had would pass to others by contract and not by the terms of her will. Her I.R.A. and company pension plan would pass to those she named as her designated beneficiaries, as would her employer sponsored group life insurance policy. Still, I told her, writing a will might be a good idea as it would then be in place when she acquired additional assets that would be in her name alone and not pass through the probate court system.

In addition, in the Will she would have the ability to designate who would serve as her Executor or Personal Representative: the person or institution that would be in charge of handling her affairs, collecting her assets, and making sure her wishes were attended to.

Despite her young age and good health, I felt it was important for Emily to put other estate planning documents in place – her health care proxy, living will and durable power of attorney. I suggested she also review her disability insurance to make sure that if she lost the capacity to work, she would still get some income.

Case Study 2: Genevieve, 49 years old, single.

About three years ago, Genevieve, a very driven career woman who had amassed significant assets, came to my office to "put her affairs in order." Her net worth exceeded $6,000,000 and there was no one in particular she wanted to leave it to. She did not have children. The members of her family were all self-sufficient, and she felt that although she could leave them her assets, she would not be filling any need in doing so. The more we spoke the more it became clear that she wanted to do something that would leave a legacy – something that would leave a mark on the world and be connected to her long after she was no longer around.

We discussed the different ways to leave assets to charities, and Genevieve had some very specific ideas. She felt that teaching today is a profession that is not as admired as it was in years past. She wanted to do something that would reward those who wanted to teach and keep them motivated and interested in their careers. She decided to endow a fund at her death at a major teaching university that would provide a semester sabbatical to a professor, selected by a committee, who wanted to enhance his or her educational training by doing something completely different – going to Europe and studying art, going to Africa on a safari, or whatever. She listed many different ideas. Her goal was to offer a teacher – who otherwise might not have not been able to afford it –a chance to see things from a different perspective. The teacher would be required to present a short paper and presentation at the end of the sabbatical on how the experience expanded his or her ability to teach.

An obvious side benefit to this was that she could avoid the estate tax bite. Instead of giving the federal and state governments the power to decide what to do with her hard earned assets, she could make the decision herself. Her money would contribute to a societal goal she believed in. Genevieve became so excited by this idea that she began negotiations with the teaching university, and finally decided to begin funding project right away from her annual income, and then have significant additional capital be added to it at her death through her estate planning documents.

Case Study 3: Beatrice, 60 years old, single

Beatrice, an attractive woman who had never married and had no children, had heard a lot about trusts and wondered if she should be doing more sophisticated planning than the simple will she had put together ten years earlier.

As we discussed her goals and objectives, she explained that she had lived with and taken care of her elderly parents for most of her adult life. Beatrice had a brother, John, a sister,

Sarah, (both of whom were married) and four nieces and nephews. She was particularly fond of one niece, Barbara, but she did not want to favor Barbara over the others.

Both John and Sarah were holding their own financially so she was not overly concerned about having to helpout any relative financially. She was very concerned, though, about who would take care of her when she grew older if she became sick. Caring for her elderly parents had made her very sensitive about this issue. She did not want to be a burden to anyone, yet she wanted to know that there was some provision for her care.

Since she was alone, I felt that her primary goal should be to provide for herself. My rule of thumb is to follow the instructions they give you on an airplane: "Should there be a problem, first put your oxygen mask on, and then put the mask on your minor children." In other words, only by taking care of yourself first will you be able to help someone else. When you are alone, it can be very difficult to know whom to trust and who will consistently be able to be there for you. Nieces and nephews often have their own lives, their own children, their own stresses and strains. They also may have their hands full caring for their own elderly parents.

Beatrice understood that and did not want to burden them. A key part of her overall security was to explore the purchase of a long term care policy – one that would allow her to remain at home, but have care brought in if she needed assistance. I explained that she should sit down with a long term care specialist as the policies can be very confusing. The specialist would give her some limited medical tests and take stock of her medical history and the medical history of various members of her family. On the basis of all of that information the insurance company would decide how much to charge her for a policy.

I told her a long term care policy would cost less at her relatively young age than if she waited until later when health issues could affect her insurability. She was worried that her own health had not been perfect, but I assured her that very few people over the age of 40 have perfect health.

What is more, the types of illnesses and diseases that may affect her ability to obtain life insurance at a good price (heart attack, cancer) do not affect the pricing of long term care policies. Long term care insurance companies tend to focus on illnesses whose victims may live a very long time but require constant custodial care, illnesses like Alzheimer's, or stroke.

We also talked about putting legal mechanisms in place so that if she became disabled or incapacitated, someone else could write her checks out, make deposits and keep her life going financially. I explained that if she lost capacity and did put these legal mechanisms in place, then someone would have to petition the court for legal permission to take charge of her affairs, and that would be expensive and time consuming.

Instead we could put in place a durable power of attorney in which she could grant one or more of her relatives the authority to handle her financial affairs. When I explained to her that the document would be in effect when she signed it and it would continue through any disability or incapacity she may have, she became concerned. She wanted a document that would become effective *only if* she became disabled or incapacitated.

I told her there was such a document - a "springing durable power of attorney"- but the problem with it was that it required a physician to certify that she was disabled and could not attend to her own financial affairs. And, since most doctors do not want to take the responsibility for such decisions themselves, they usually ask a court to make the decision.

She seemed concerned about entrusting one family member with such a difficult decision. I suggested that she consider other options —such as naming two family members and mandating that both signatures would be required, or naming a major financial institution as her agent.

I also suggested that she consider establishing a revocable, or living trust and that she transfer most of her assets into it. While she was alive and competent she would be totally in charge of the trust and any assets it held. The trust document would be fairly specific on who would have the authority to handle her affairs if she were no longer able to do so.

I explained that with a durable power of attorney, the person designated as your agent can do anything he or she wishes with your assets, as if she were you. A revocable trust, on the other hand, is more specific about how the assets can be used, how they should be invested, who the trustees are who would have the authority to distribute funds, and for what purposes they could be distributed.

While Beatrice was alive and competent, all of those choices would be hers. The point of the trust was to make adequate provisions for what would happen if she got to a point where she was no longer able to take care of her own financial affairs because of disability or death. I also explained that trusts have been around a very long time, and there are laws in each state that govern the rights, duties and obligations of the trustee.

For many people, both a durable power of attorney and a trust are used in tandem. That is because not all assets can be retitled into a trust during your lifetime. Beatrice was a history teacher. She had pension benefits. She also had an IRA account. These types of assets cannot be transferred into a trust. Should she become disabled, even if all of her other assets were held in trust, the pension and the IRA would be frozen and inaccessible in the event of her disability or incapacity as she is the only person who has the legal authority to transact those assets.

If she named someone as her agent under the durable power of attorney then that person would have the authority to handle the assets that were not in the trust, and the trustee (who may be the same person) would have the authority to handle the assets held in the trust.

Beatrice found all of this quite confusing and difficult to follow. I laughed and told her that the concept of having so many different sources of authority to handle all that she is currently handling is a concept most people initially struggle with, but there are good reasons for each document and the way that they work together.

We also discussed two more documents for her to consider implementing during her lifetime- the health care proxy and the living will. In the health care proxy she wanted to name her sister, Sarah, who was a nurse, to make any medical decisions for her if she was not able to make them herself.

Under the law of almost every state only one person can be named to serve in that capacity at any time – although more than one person can be named successively. She told me that she wanted to really give some thought as to who would serve if Sarah was unable to. I told her I certainly understood that. It was a very difficult responsibility and not everyone is comfortable doing it. I also told her that she may want to put the person she was most comfortable with down for now and change it later, and I reminded her that all of the documents we discussed during that consultation could be changed, amended or revoked at any time.

I asked her if she wanted to also sign a living will, which differs slightly from a health care proxy. Under the health care proxy, Sarah would have the authority to do everything from check on Beatrice's medical records to consider whether or not to terminate life support. A living will would help Sarah do all that by specifying what Beatrice's wishes are. If Beatrice felt strongly that she did not want to be maintained on life support, for example, then signing a living will, which stated that, would make it easier for Sarah to make that type of decision.

I stressed how important it was for Beatrice to discuss all of this with Sarah, since frequently in a crisis there is no time to have that type of discussion.

I brought up two more points I thought she should consider. The first was that since her assets were less than $1,500,000, there would not be any federal estate tax due and although there would be a state estate tax due, it would not be worth worrying about or planning around. She was very relieved to hear that.

The second was that she had to decide who would receive her assets at her death. She told me that she loved all of her family members equally and did not want to favor or slight anyone. Her real goal, she said, was to make sure that education was always available to whichever relative needed it. She had been a teacher her entire career, and the value of education was very important to her.

I suggested setting up a trust for the education of her nieces and nephews and their children and the education of subsequent generations. That excited her. She wanted to know how it would work.

I told her we could just specify that the funds in the revocable trust be used for tuition and related expenses (as determined by a committee of trustees) for family members until the funds ran out.

The more we talked about this idea, the more interested she became in it. Along the same lines I thought she should also consider, at her death, taking some of her assets and funding a scholarship in her family name at the school she had taught at for so many years. I explained she could make that type of scholarship available to students according to any criteria she selected –to the student who wanted to make education a career and wrote the best history paper, for example, or the student who wanted to go to college and have history as a major, or whatever she desired.

Beatrice began to understand that estate planning encompassed far more than executing a will. She left my office thinking about her affairs in a whole new way.

Strategies for the Single Woman:

1. Put in place the legal documents (health care proxy, durable power of attorney, living will) that will protect you if you become disabled or incapacitated.

2. Make sure you have appropriate disability and long term care insurance.

3. Be creative and flexible in arranging your affairs so that you will maintain control of your assets during your lifetime and provide for those persons or institutions you care about at your death.

4. Name a person, team of people, or a financial institution to take over if you are disabled so that you will be continuously protected.

5. Make sure that your Will has been updated to reflect your current desires and that you have selected an appropriate Executor or Personal Representative.

6. Consider establishing a living trust. While not for everyone, a Living Trust can be a powerful tool to provide for both estate management if you are incapacitated and estate distribution if you die.

7. Review the Primary and Secondary Beneficiaries on your Retirement Plans and Life Insurance Policies. Make sure that they are correctly filled out so that your assets are going where you intend.

8. If your estate exceeds the current estate tax threshold consider making lifetime gifts (to individuals or charities). Consider the enormous benefits your contributions might bring to churches, religious organizations, schools, hospitals, museums, scholarship funds, and your favorite causes or organizations.

9. Review, revise and update your estate plan at least every five years and as soon as your circumstances change.

10. Preplan and perhaps prepay your funeral so that you know that your wishes will be carried out.

CHAPTER SIX

Married Woman

"Newlyweds become oldyweds, and oldyweds are the reasons that families work."
–AUTHOR UNKNOWN

UNLIKE SINGLE AND DIVORCED WOMEN, MARRIED WOMEN DON'T HAVE TO DO THEIR estate planning all by themselves. They have a *partner* in this process. While that may feel comforting, it can also create problems.

Often, but not always, it is more difficult for women than it is for men to take charge of the family's estate planning: to *own* this responsibility. In many marriages the husband is still more accustomed to making business decisions and dealing with advisors, attorneys, accountants, and financial planners. As a result, the wife may defer to her husband on estate planning… which is a shame, because, since women are still outliving men by seven years, the probabilities are *she* is the one who will either benefit or suffer from the estate planning decisions that are made.

So the first order of business for the married woman is: **Educate yourself.** Know everything there is to know about your family's finances. Be comfortable with your estate planning advisors. Ask questions. Take an active role in the creation of a family plan that assures your young children will be taken care of if something happens to you and your husband. Understand what your family's income is, what your ongoing liabilities are (mortgage payments, children's tuition). Learn how you can go about **creating enough wealth** to preserve your current lifestyle if either your income or your husband's dissipates as a result of death or disability. And know that it is never too soon to make such preparations.

About 10 years ago, a couple in their 30s with young children came to me and did an estate plan. They executed all of the appropriate documents – durable powers of attorney, health care proxies, wills and trusts. The husband was earning $100,000 a year. The wife was not working. They had modest assets. The husband was youthful and healthy – an athlete – but, just to be safe, he had taken out a life insurance policy on himself for $1,000,000. This seemed like overdoing the safety net to them – taking out this astronomical amount of life insurance they would probably never need.

But, as I pointed out, the policy was, in fact, inadequate. One million dollars of investable assets will conservatively yield $50,000 annually in income. That would not have allowed her to maintain her lifestyle and educate her children. A $3,000,000 life insurance policy would generate about $150,000 in income and would allow her to be able to do what was needed.

They took my suggestion and purchased the insurance.

And, one cold, winter night, a few years later he went out to play hockey (as he had done since he was 16) and died of a massive heart attack. No one had foreseen this. He had no history of heart issues.

If it is difficult to take estate planning issues seriously when you are young and feel in perfect health. It can be equally difficult to do so - albeit for totally different reasons - when death is imminent. When her husband was dying, Christina, a bright, educated 50 year old did not want to acknowledge to him or to herself that the end was near. When an insurance agent who was close to both her husband and his family came on the scene and suggested that her husband consolidate all of his financial assets and purchase a significant annuity to make it "easier" for his family, she thought it best not to interfere.

Her husband followed the agent's advice, naming his wife and three minor children all equal beneficiaries of the annuity contract.

This created several problems when he died. First, by not leaving most of the money to his wife, he exceeded the dollar threshold amount that could be passed on tax free, incurring an unnecessary estate tax.

Second, instead of leaving the assets to his wife to control or in trust for his children, he left them to his children, giving them outright control of their shares as soon as they turned 18. One of the sons was 16 years old and having a very difficult time adjusting to his father's death. Turning the assets over to him at the age of 18 could have been disastrous.

I explained to Christina that it was possible to become guardian of her minor children

---

Legalese Defined

Qualified Terminable Interest Property (QTIP). A trust (especially useful in second marriages where the grantor desires to provide for a second spouse, but wants the trust assets to be distributed to his/her children upon the spouse's death) established for the benefit of a spouse that qualifies for the unlimited marital deduction and controls where the trust assets pass at the surviving spouse's death.

and petition the court on their behalf to **"disclaim,"** (temporarily renounce) the amount of their inheritance that exceeded the sum that could pass to them free of estate taxes, leaving it to her instead. She hesitated at first, afraid of hurting the feelings of her husband's death-bed "advisor," but then acknowledged that handing over an extra $500,000 to the Internal Revenue Service merely because of poor planning was not in the best interest of her family and certainly not what her husband would have ever wanted.

She guaranteed that her children would receive the money at her death and purchased a life insurance policy that would be paid to them when she died so that they would not be disadvantaged by whatever life dealt her.

The court required that an independent lawyer be appointed to make sure that this was in the child's best interest. Two court proceedings and six months later, we prevailed. Although she was much relieved, Christina kept bemoaning the fact that if *only* she had known enough to ask the right questions at the right time she could have saved the family legal fees, administrative hassle and mental angst.

This is a common *if only.*

Caroline's husband, Charles, died, and when she called me after returning from a meeting with the attorneys, she was barely able to hold back tears of anger and frustration. Her husband had told her she would be receiving most of his fortune, because money left to a spouse is exempt from estate taxes when the first spouse dies. And, in fact, she had received most of his fortune.

But what she and her husband had failed to understand in their meetings with the estate planners was that the money had not been left outright to her. Instead it was put into a trust — a **Q-TIP (Qualified Terminable Interest in Property)** trust. And although this special type of marital trust makes the wealth that is transferred exempt from federal estate taxes, it can also drastically limit the surviving spouse's use of the funds.

Caroline admitted she hadn't been paying much attention when she'd sat through the estate planning discussions with Charles and his attorneys, and frankly, neither had Charles. They had relied on their legal advisors. All Charles and Caroline understood was that the estate taxes would be deferred until both of them died and that Caroline was going to be the primary beneficiary of all of Charles's assets.

But it turned out that Charles — through a number of conditions — had inadvertently limited Caroline's use of what she had always considered "their money" and now "her money." The trustees named by her husband in the trust document to manage the QTIP trust told her she would be entitled to all of the net income from the trust – the dividends and interest - after their fee was paid. They asked her to submit a budget, so they could determine what her lifestyle was and they could arrange a monthly "allowance" to be paid from the trust. She would have to "justify" any larger withdrawals. They would review any requests she made, and they had the right to say no.

Caroline was shocked. Her husband had not restricted her access to money when he was alive and she could not believe he was - indirectly – doing it in death. She was angry at Charles for not having understood this, and she was angry at herself for not asking more questions during the planning process. Had the attorneys who drafted the documents imposed their own value system and given them standard, off-the-shelf documents?

The attorneys told her that as a spouse who is a beneficiary but not also a trustee, she had no voice in the trust decisions. One of the trustees was the head of an investment company, and the trustees selected his company to manage the trust funds. She thought for sure she could do better on her own, using her own investment adviser – someone she and Charles had both invested financial assets with over the past few years.

Sorry, the attorneys told her, the terms of the trust provided that *the trustees,* not the widow, would choose the investment manager.

But, she asked, couldn't she have been named a trustee, even though she was a beneficiary of the trust?

Yes, they told her, but she and Charles had never brought that up in the discussions during the estate planning process.

Caroline was also told that she couldn't choose where the money would go at her death. This QTIP trust already controlled that decision, and there was nothing she could do to change things. She and Charles had selected beneficiaries who would receive the balance of the trust after both their deaths, and those beneficiaries were in both documents.

But when they had made those choices, they had naively thought that was what would happen if they died together! Why, one of the beneficiaries they had selected had not even shown up at her husband's funeral! Surely, Caroline had argued, she should be able to remove him as a beneficiary.

No, the attorneys said, that was not possible.

When I reviewed the trust, I was shocked to discover that Caroline did not even have the right to remove the Trustees and appoint new ones. We settled on a course of negotiation and, over time, we were able to open up a line of communication with the trustees and achieve better results for her than the attorneys and trustees had initially offered.

The lesson that Caroline and Charles had only half learned in the estate planning meetings was that by leaving assets to each other they could defer paying estate taxes until both of them died. What was not clearly explained to them was the concept of the two trust system, that leaving assets in trust does not reduce the amount of estate taxes that will eventually be due. It simply defers the tax and in return, if the trusts are not drafted properly, it may limit the surviving spouse's access to the funds.

To understand this Caroline and Charles should have been told that in 1981, Congress changed federal estate-tax law creating an **unlimited marital deduction** which allows one spouse to transfer all assets to a surviving spouse without incurring either estate or gift taxes. No estate taxes have to be paid until after the surviving spouse passes away. At first glance, this seems the ideal estate-planning tool to avoid federal estate taxes, if you have a large enough estate. But in fact, it is just a postponement: If you leave everything to your spouse, the estate could be subject to huge taxes when the second spouse dies - owning everything and having just one estate tax deduction, not two. As discussed previously in this book, for the years 2011 and 2012 the federal estate tax exemption is $5,000,000 per person. It is not yet clear what will happen after 2012 – it is possible that the exemptions will revert to pre-2010 exemption levels and that the federal estate tax rate after 2012 will climb back up to the prior 45 level. Even if your combined estates are less than the federal estate tax exemption thresholds, in many states there is a state estate tax that will be due and which should be considered.

For these reasons estate planning attorneys typically plan for two trusts to be created at the death of the first spouse. In most cases these are "revocable trusts" – trusts husband and wife can change, amend or revoke during their lifetime.

At the death of the first spouse, that person's revocable trust breaks into two trusts. The first trust, commonly known as the family trust or credit shelter trust, receives assets in the amount of the estate tax exemption (which is $5,000,000 under the current law). This "by-pass trust" takes advantage of the individual's estate-tax exemption. Typically, these trusts have been drafted so that the spouse and the children are permissible beneficiaries of the trust, but the spouse is allowed to withdraw income or even dip into the principal of that trust if he or she needs to. With the significant increase in the federal exemption, it is possible that the funding language in the trust will drop most of the assets of the first spouse to die into this bypass trust. Most couples do not want the children to be on equal footing with the surviving spouse during the surviving spouse's lifetime and would instead prefer that children receive assets only when the surviving spouse decides it is a good idea to gift it to them or when both spouses die. Therefore, if you are married and your estate plan includes a bypass trust it is critical that you review its provisions with your estate planning attorney and make an informed decision as to who the beneficiary of the bypass trust should be during the surviving spouse's lifetime. In most states the spouse can be the trustee of this trust too. That is an important decision and should be carefully reviewed. It is the trustee who has the legal right to access information from the financial institutions and who will make decisions on whether assets should be maintained or sold.

The second trust is known as the "marital trust." The most popular form of marital trust these days is the QTIP trust – the trust that Charles and Caroline unwittingly established as part of their estate plan. After the credit shelter trust is funded with the estate tax exemption amount, the rest of the assets go into the marital trust. For wealthy individuals this can be most of that person's net worth.

What most people do not understand when they are going through the estate planning process is that there is absolutely no tax reason to keep this trust in place. The same tax deferral will occur if the money is left outright to the surviving spouse with no restrictions. The marital trust is set up *for control reasons,* not for tax reasons. I'm not saying all control reasons are bad. I'm just saying the decision on how much control to put in place should be thought through very carefully, and the consequences understood by both partners, during the planning process.

Valid reasons for creating a marital trust include protecting the money from the surviving spouse's creditors and keeping the assets separate, in case the surviving spouse remarries. In the case of a second marriage, a QTIP marital trust can protect the surviving spouse financially for his or her lifetime and guarantee that the children of the first marriage do not lose their share of the estate.

A QTIP trust is often used when attorneys are overprotective of their clients, have little respect for the financial abilities of the surviving spouse, or when a spouse seeks to exert continued control, even from the grave. Whatever the motivation, any attorney who creates such a plan without fully explaining its restrictions to both spouses has created an ethical conflict of interest.

But at the same time, any spouse who does not participate in the estate planning process and get understandable answers to all the questions on her mind may very well agree to restrictions she is not aware of until it is too late to change them. Married women must think through their goals ahead of time, and make sure those goals are achieved.

Strategies for the Married Woman:

1. Know what assets are in your name, what assets are in your husband's name, what assets are held jointly.

2. Know who the primary and secondary beneficiaries are of any life insurance policy on your life and your husband's life.

3. Know who the primary and secondary beneficiaries are of any retirement plans, I.R.A.s, 401(k)s or annuities on your life and your husband's life.

4. Know what your household assets are and what your household income is.

5. Be sure you and your husband have durable powers of attorney, health care proxies, wills and trusts.

6. Know who is named Executor in both of your estate planning documents, and who is named Trustee.

7. Know what your income will be if your husband becomes disabled and his salary does not continue to be paid to support the family. If appropriate explore the purchase of disability insurance.

8. Know what you will receive if your husband predeceases you and whether you will receive those assets outright or in trust, what debt exists and how it will be paid, and what liquid assets will be available to pay bills, debts, and mortgages.

9. Know what your income will be if your husband predeceases you and his income is no longer available and how you will be able to educate your children.

10. Know who the family advisors are (lawyer, accountant, financial planner, life insurance professional, investment advisor, business advisor) and to whom you can turn if you need assistance.

11. Explore the purchase of long term care insurance for you and your spouse.

12. Designate a guardian and a trustee for your minor children in the event of your and your husband's deaths, and decide at what age your children should receive funds.

13. Review your property and casualty insurance to make sure that the appropriate levels of insurance are in place and consider purchasing umbrella liability coverage.

CHAPTER SEVEN

Divorced Woman

"I'm tired of love: I'm still more tired of rhyme.
But money gives me pleasure all the time."
–HILLAIRE BELLOC

FOR MOST WOMEN, DIVORCE IS ONE OF THE MOST STRESSFUL AND UNPLEASANT experiences in life. Emotions run high. Solutions are scarce. Money is tight. Legal bills are exorbitant. It is not the best time to make well thought-out decisions.

Sally, a 38 year old wife and mother came to me because she was convinced her husband was going to divorce her and she wanted to know how she could protect herself from an estate planning point of view. She was not sure where their assets were held, who their financial advisors were, or what their estate planning documents provided. I encouraged her to ask her husband, Tom, these questions, but she was concerned that if she did that, it would trigger action.

I asked her if she remembered signing a durable power of attorney in which she would have given her husband the full authority to handle her financial affairs without asking her permission first. She was not sure. She just remembered going to the law office and signing the documents that were put in front of her without any questions. I asked her if they owned joint investment assets where only one person's signature would be required to make a transaction, write a check, withdraw funds, change an investment advisor, etc. She said she was not sure as she had not been directly involved with the investments either.

I told her to get copies of the last three years of their income tax returns. This, I've found, is the best way to begin figuring out the financial road map. I also told her to peruse the check book for evidence of life insurance premium payments, see if the safe deposit box has the estate planning documents in it, and to find the deed to the house.

She gathered together as much of the information as she could and came in to review it.

We put together a pro forma financial statement of our best guess of what the assets were, the assets she could access, the assets that would be inaccessible and the assets her husband could move without her permission. This gave her a starting point to think about what steps she should take to secure her financial future –whether she was married or divorced. It gave her the power to understand the position she would be negotiating from if, in fact, her husband did serve her with divorce papers.

Jill, a woman of 54, made an appointment to come see me with her husband, Brian, to discuss their estate plan. As a beginning part of this process I send out a questionnaire and ask potential new clients to pull together their financial information and to bring that information, along with copies of their current estate planning documents, to the initial meeting. Jill and Brian came in and had an in-depth two hour session.

Five minutes after leaving my office Jill called me from her cell phone in the lobby and told me they would not be proceeding. She had set up the appointment to obtain a complete picture of their finances before commencing a divorce action, and she figured that starting the estate planning process was cheaper than years of document production and discovery.

I recommend neither Sally nor Jill's course of action. Each underscores, in fact, how important it is to understand what your finances are and how your estate planning works *long before the marriage falls apart.*

If, however, that did not happen, and now you are on the threshold of legal action, you should be thinking about where your vulnerabilities are and how to shore up your defenses.

If you and your husband did sign durable powers of attorney, then you probably want to revoke yours. (This can be difficult to do. A review of the language in the durable power of attorney should explain how to do so. All documents are different. You may also want to file that revocation with all the financial institutions you currently have assets at as well as the Registry of Deeds for the county in which you live. That should put third persons on notice that a revocation is in place. But be prepared to deal with the consequences of doing this. Obviously, when you put the revocation of the durable power of attorney on record everywhere that your financial assets are held, chances are your spouse will find out.

For many couples, qualified pension plans and IRAs are significant assets. Under ERISA once you are married for one year, neither spouse can change or direct any qualified plan assets to anyone (including a trust for the spouse's benefit) without the spouse's written authorization. That means if your husband holds a significant qualified plan benefit and does not name you as the primary beneficiary and does not have your written permission, then the designation of the person other than you is not valid and if he dies you will receive the asset. Unfortunately, if you gave your consent once – for example to have the proceeds paid to a trust for your benefit – that consent is considered to have been given and he can change the beneficiary again to someone else – for example the children directly – without obtaining your written consent again. The theory behind this is that once you agree in writing that it is OK not to be the beneficiary, it does not matter who is the beneficiary.

ERISA covers qualified plans, but it does not cover IRAs. Either spouse can change the primary beneficiary of the IRA without the written permission of the other spouse.

From a health care point of view the law in most states provides that if you have executed a health care proxy or durable power of attorney for health care purposes and legal action is filed to separate or divorce, then that constitutes a revocation of your spouse having the right to make medical decisions on your behalf. Obviously the reasoning behind this is that a hostile spouse should not be able to decide your course of medical treatment or whether you live or die.

Life insurance is tricky for the divorcing. In many states you cannot change the designated beneficiary of a life insurance policy you own once a court action has begun. It is routine to obtain a court order that freezes the policies as is. In some states, New Jersey, for instance, there is a 90 day look back and any changes to life insurance beneficiary designations made within 90 days of filing an action for divorce are disregarded. Obviously, how you react to these laws depends on which side of the fence you are sitting on. If you do not want your spouse to be named as the beneficiary of your life insurance policy, then that should be changed well in advance of any legal action. If you want to make sure that you are maintained as the beneficiary of your husband's life insurance policy, then you want to be sure to seek a court order which will keep that in effect.

If either you or your husband owns stock in a family or closely held business then take a look at the stockholders agreement. Many provide that if the stockholder is involved in a legal action for separation or divorce, the other shareholders or partners have the right to buy the interest of the divorcing shareholder. Any such agreement should be carefully reviewed and analyzed to quantify any possible risks before a complaint is filed. If there are significant negative consequences that will ensue if a complaint for divorce is filed, a renegotiation of the agreement might be warranted. Certainly, if filing a divorce complaint might bring undesired economic results, you want to know that and think through the consequences before starting any action. Think about both you and your husband's relationship with the other owners. Are they family members? How will they react? Will those in power see this as an opportunity to deprive your family of the ownership of the stock? Will a divestiture of that stock affect your childrens' ability to enter into the business?

Frequently, in a divorce proceeding after a long term marriage, the judge will order alimony payments.   If your husband is ordered to pay alimony, you may want to ask him to establish what is known as **an alimony trust** as part of the divorce agreement, where he transfers cash, investment assets or business assets into a trust ahead of time, and that trust then provides the required alimony payments when they are due. It is a way of making sure alimony payments will not be jeopardized by your spouse's having to pay off creditors or other financial problems. It also enables you to cut the ties and not have to either deal with your former spouse or worry about whether his check will arrive on time.

Let's say your husband puts $1,000,000 into an alimony trust with the agreement that the trust will pay you $50,000 in a combination of alimony and child support annually until your child hits 18. You can also decide, as part of the divorce decree, that the trust will pay the premiums on a life insurance policy on your soon-to-be-ex-husband, a policy which will list you as beneficiary. The purpose of this is to make sure child support or alimony continues if your husband dies before his obligation is satisfied. After he meets those obligations, he can change the beneficiary on his life insurance policy to someone else. If the assets in the trust appreciate and the income exceeds the amount needed for alimony or child support, then your husband will not have to pay taxes on any part of the appreciation he used to pay out alimony or child support, but anything over and above that he will pay taxes on.

A divorce also obviously affects spousal estate rights. In virtually every state, a married spouse is entitled to a percentage of her husband's assets even if she is omitted from her husband's will. This is known as an elective share, or a forced share. In most states this is at least one-third of the deceased spouse's assets. When divorced the only rights that the former spouse has to assets are whatever court order states— in most cases that will only include a life insurance policy to cover unpaid alimony or child support.

If minor children are involved, then a key part of the estate planning process for a divorced woman is deciding whom to choose as the children's guardian of the person – normally the father of the children, or ex-husband - and whom to choose as guardian of the child's property. That person will be put in charge of the children's money – frequently *not* the guardian of the person if you and your ex-husband have an estranged relationship. It may be one thing to have the child's father be the guardian of the person and another to have your ex-husband decide how to spend your money after your death.

Making such decisions is an emotionally charged process for most parents, and for di-

----

Legalese Defined

Alimony Trust: A trust established as part of the divorce agreement, into which cash, investment assets or business assets are transferred before the alimony payments are due. The trust then pays out the required amount of money for the alimony payments.

vorcing parents it can be a lightening rod. In many cases, the ex-husband/parent will have continuing responsibility to pay for the child's care, and the ex-wife will want to be assured that if she dies, the money that she has set aside for the children will *not* be used by the ex-husband to discharge his parental obligations, but instead will be saved, invested, and put aside for later goals.

For this reason the person you choose to be in charge of the children's funds is important. Often a family friend will be chosen or a major financial institution in the trust business who is accustomed to dealing with these issues.

Some women in this type of situation will put an affirmative statement in wills and trusts that under no circumstances shall the ex-husband or any subsequent spouse or partner he may have ever serve as a trustee of any trusts that the woman establishes.

After the divorce it is important to make sure that you follow up and comply with any of the court orders. It is also important to make sure that your husband complies with any of his obligations. Post divorce you should execute new estate planning documents – a new durable power of attorney, health care proxy, will and trust - to bring your objectives into focus with your current objectives. When doing that make sure that you have also coordinated the designated beneficiaries of your life insurance policies and retirement plan benefits. If they are still made payable to an ex-spouse after the divorce and you die he may collect them.

Strategies for the Divorced Woman:

1. Understand the terms of your divorce agreement, what your ex-husband is obligated to pay for alimony and child support and whether or not his obligation to pay is ordered to be backed up by a life insurance policy on his life.

2. If it is backed up by a life insurance policy, check each year to make sure the premiums are paid and that the policy remains in force.

3. Revise your estate planning documents in light of your divorce to reflect the appropriate parties to serve as attorney under your power of attorney, agent under your health care proxy, executor under your will and trustee under any trust.

4. Make sure your ex-husband is not still the beneficiary of your estate plan and revise the primary and secondary beneficiaries of your life insurance, IRA, annuities, retirement planning assets, etc. to remove your ex-husband from those designations.

CHAPTER EIGHT

Re-Married Woman

"In order to plan your future wisely, it is necessary that you understand and appreciate your past."
-JO COUDERT

SALLY, A 57-YEAR-OLD PEDIATRIC NURSE WITH A 13-YEAR-OLD SON FELL IN LOVE WITH TED, a retired doctor 20 years her senior with three children in their 40s. Sally and her son moved into Ted's house to test whether or not they could all live together. Things went very well and Sally and Ted married three years later.

Sally and Ted *meant* to put their legal affairs in order before tying the knot, but they were so busy integrating households, making sure her son adjusted to his new stepfather, working, and traveling, they never got around to estate planning.

Two years after the marriage Ted dropped dead of a heart attack. Sally was understandably devastated. Ted's children, who viewed Sally as a gold digger entering their father's life when he was susceptible to a younger woman's charms, wanted to immediately evict her from his home. Ted and their mother had lived there for 35 years, and the children viewed the house as their house, not Sally's.

They went to a lawyer to find out how to evict her and how to restrain her from removing or touching any of the house's personal effects. The children petitioned the court to be named Administrators of Ted's estate (since he did not have a Will).

Sally was served with the papers just after the funeral and called my office for an emergency appointment to find out if she had any role to play in her husband's affairs, what length of time she would be allowed to stay in the house, and what her legal rights to other assets would be.

We cross petitioned the court to have Sally appointed to administer her husband's affairs. Envisioning a major battle brewing, the judge appointed an independent lawyer rather than putting any family member in charge. Most of Ted's assets were paid to his children, since he had never gotten around to making anything payable to Sally. Many months later, after huge legal fees were paid to the children's attorney, Sally's attorney and the independent attorney who had to referee the probate administration, a settlement among all parties was reached. No one was happy with the result. Sally was very mad at Ted for leaving her unprotected and mad at herself for not being more assertive about forcing the issue sooner.

When a woman enters into a second marriage, she usually has assets that are hers, assets she has either earned or inherited. She also may have new vulnerabilities as she gives up one lifestyle for another and merges property. Protecting herself and her assets is an important part of her estate plan, especially if she has children from a prior marriage. For these reasons, prior to remarriage, many women consider a **prenuptial** - or *ante nuptial* - **agreement.**

Prenuptial agreements are not new. The court records show that a James Young and a Susan Huffman entered into a premarital agreement in Page County, Virginia in 1844. Prenuptials are also not just for celebrity couples like Jackie Kennedy and Aristotle Onassis, Michael Douglas and Catherine Zeta- Jones, Madonna and Guy Ritchie and Paul McCartney and Heather Mills. Increasing numbers of women today remarrying in their 30s, 40s, 50s, 60s, 70s and 80s consider these agreements an important part of secure financial planning.

That's because a prenuptial agreement can safeguard assets, protect family members, keep a business in the family, and in certain circumstances, even cover such specific details as how the mortgage and daily expenses are to be are to be paid if and when a marriage ends. They can be as broad or as limited as you and your fiancée decide.

Are you a little concerned about being saddled with your fiancé's business debts? Or with the demands of his ex-wife? Are you worried about how much you will have to contribute to the support of his children? A well-drafted prenuptial agreement can handle all of these issues. If you are giving up a career or a lucrative job to get married, a prenuptial agreement can also set forth compensation for your sacrifice if the marriage fails.

Tom was a really successful businessman, and one of the reasons that he and Stephanie, 42, hit it off so well was that they both loved to travel. After Tom proposed, however, Stephanie realized his business mandated that he be on the road a lot, and if she went along with him, as he wanted her to, she would have to quit her job. The traveling he had in mind far exceeded her allowable vacations.

She did not want to appear greedy but she was afraid to quit her job without the assurance of some financial protection. What if something happened to him and she was left without a means of support? She wanted to be sure she would always have a roof over her head and sufficient cash flow to support herself.

Tom understood the concept, but had trouble deciding how much she should receive.

If they married and he died within a year, for example, Stephanie would be able to re-enter the work force fairly easily, and he felt if their marriage was that short, a significant amount of his net worth should go to his children from his prior marriage.

In the end they decided Tom should buy a $2,000,000 life insurance policy for a ten year term, which would be payable to Stephanie, and they put a clause in the prenuptial agreement that after the ten year mark, if they were still married, she would be entitled to one-third of his estate and, at the 20 year mark, to one-half of his estate.

Stephanie and Tom's decision to address the **division of assets at various stages in the marriage** is fairly common. Many prenuptial agreements specify that if the marriage lasts less than two years, the division may be minimal or nonexistent, but that the payout portion will increase as the length of the marriage increases.

A prenuptial can address the issue of **alimony** in the case of divorce, assuring the wealthier spouse that the financial impact of a divorce will be controlled, and at the same time assuring the less wealthy spouse that she or he will be provided for adequately.

Without a prenuptial agreement in place it is up to the laws of the state in which you are domiciled (and, in certain cases, the states in which you own real estate) to determine what assets or income your spouse is entitled to keep in a divorce and which assets will pass to your spouse when you die. In most states, without a prenuptial agreement, a surviving spouse has the right to inherit one-third to one-half of your probate assets.

A prenuptial agreement can override that and make sure that the property you owned prior to the marriage is given to your children from your prior marriage at your death. It can also specify that assets you do decide to leave to your spouse will not be left outright, but will remain in trust for the duration of the spouse's lifetime, and then pass to the children when both of you die.

If you live in one of the nine **community property states** – Arizona, California, Idaho, Louisiana, Nevada, New Mexico, Texas, Washington or Wisconsin – without a prenuptial agreement the law says that property accumulated during the marriage will be equally divided. In all other **"equitable distribution states,"** assets are divided according to what a judge determines to be fair or equitable (which does not necessarily mean equal). In making that decision the judge takes into consideration factors such as the length of the marriage, whether or not there are children, and the couple's age, health, and job skills. Alaska is different. It is an equitable distribution state but allows the parties to enter into a community property agreement.

Typically, a prenuptial agreement will address several **categories of assets:** those assets acquired and owned prior to the date of marriage, all income and appreciation on property owned and acquired prior to the marriage, all property earned and acquired by either spouse during the marriage, all appreciation in the value of assets acquired during the marriage, and all assets received by gift or inheritance during the marriage.

If each party has assets of comparable value, it may make sense to establish the **what is mine is mine and what is your is yours** type of agreement, specifying that the assets I bring to this marriage (and any appreciation during the course of the marriage on those assets) is mine, the assets you bring to the marriage (and any appreciation during the course of the marriage on those assets) is yours. Any assets we acquire together during the marriage will be put in joint names and will pass to the surviving spouse at death – or be split equally between us if we divorce.

A mine is mine and yours is yours agreement may not be fair if one party entering in the marriage has very little net worth. In that type of case a smart move may be to guarantee the less wealthy a specific amount of money, either when the contract is entered into or when the marriage ends. That helps make the agreement enforceable.

After re-marrying, you may decide to live together in your home, or in his home. You may both sell your homes and purchase a new one together. In second marriage situations the home is an asset with strong emotions… and who has the title is an important issue to address in a prenuptial agreement. In many states, **ownership** of a primary residence is **based on survivorship:** If one spouse dies, the ownership passes by law to the surviving spouse. In a second marriage, that could mean that the children of the first spouse to die lose inheritance rights to the house they grew up in.

An alternative is for the re-marrying couple to hold the property as **tenants in common,** a form of joint ownership without a survivorship right. Each person's age in the home would pass through his or her will (or trust if probate had been avoided) to those persons that the spouse has selected. In such situations it's common to have the deceased spouse's interest in the home held in trust for the duration of the surviving spouse's life, then at the death of both of them the home would pass to the deceased spouse's children. The surviving spouse could even be the sole trustee during his or her lifetime, which gives him or her the flexibility to sell the home and reinvest the proceeds in a smaller condominium or a home in another state. It also guarantees that although the surviving spouse has that flexibility, at the death of both spouses whatever the assets have been invested in – the current home, proceeds of the sale of the home or a new home - will pass under the terms of the deceased spouse's estate plan to his or her children.

A pension plan or retirement planning asset is usually a major component of a woman's financial picture. For that reason, it is common to include a clause in the prenuptial agreement that requires the new spouse to waive his or her interest in the retirement plan. That is because under federal law after a couple has been married for one year, the spouse is deemed the beneficiary of the retirement plan (even if someone else had previously been named beneficiary) unless the spouse designated someone else or a trust as the beneficiary some time *after the marriage.*

The goal of the law, of course, is to protect the spouse and provide him or her with the retirement asset. But it is tricky, because once the spouse signs off on the benefit and consents to designate someone else as the recipient, the name of the beneficiary can be changed again without the consent of subsequent beneficiaries, on the theory that once the spouse agrees that it is OK not to receive that asset, it no longer matters who receives it.

There are certain issues that **cannot be legally agreed to in a prenuptial agreement.** For example, parties cannot contract what child support would be if the marriage ends in divorce. Under the current law, they also can't contract for child related issues such as custody or visitation. Many parties will, however, include language which states their intent on those issues when the agreement is entered into. Parties also cannot stipulate that they will not be responsible for their new spouse's medical care. That is against public policy.

Prenuptial agreements can be challenged –at the time of divorce and at death. One of the key issues the court considers in reviewing the agreement's validity is how honest the parties were in disclosing their finances. After all, a party to an agreement can only *knowingly* waive rights to an asset if she has sufficient information about what the asset's true value is. "Assets" include tangibles like heirlooms, houses, and finances and intangibles like intellectual properties, copyrights, royalties, medical licenses, and law degrees.

The court also considers whether both parties had competent legal counsel. Director Steven Spielberg's now ex-wife, Amy Irving, walked away with half their net worth because their prenuptial agreement was scribbled on a napkin, and she was not represented by an attorney.

The court will also consider whether or not the party was under duress when the agreement was signed, and "duress" can be something as simple as the fact that the prenuptial agreement was signed so close to the wedding date that a signing party did not have time to consider the consequences of the agreement. When Donald Trump filed for divorce from Marla Maples in 1997, three months after they separated, Maples fought the prenuptial agreement that allotted her $2,000,000 in the event of a divorce on the grounds that she had

---

Legalese Defined

Tenancy in Common: A type of ownership where two or more people share a property, but not necessarily equally, and although each one has the right to use the entire property, there is no right of survivorship. Any party may petition the court for a sale of property and have the proceeds divided. At the death of one owner, the other owners do not automatically inherit.

not read the prenuptial agreement before she signed it. They settled the case without a trial and her lawyer reported in the news that Trump promised to pay her more than what was stated in the contract.

The court may also determine if there was fraud involved during the negotiation and/or signing of the agreement.

Even though it is not required in many states, the court may also usually consider whether or not each party had separate and independent counsel. If you choose to waive the right to counsel in signing a prenuptial, you might want to state that in the document – that the right to retain independent counsel was explained and understood but the party chose to proceed anyway.

Finally, in many states, an agreement can be challenged on the grounds of its not being "fair and reasonable." This can be a two pronged test: 1) whether the agreement was fair and reasonable when the marriage was entered into and 2) whether the agreement is fair and reasonable when the marriage terminates. In such cases the judge is asked to determine whether one spouse took advantage of the other.

Even though prenuptial agreements can be challenged, the trend in case law is to uphold the agreement. In California, for example, the Supreme Court unanimously upheld the premarital contract between San Francisco baseball star Barry Bonds and his wife, Sun. The couple met in Montreal in 1987 when Bonds was a fledgling baseball player for the Pittsburgh Pirates and his wife was studying to be a beautician. They were both 23 years old. They courted for three months and became engaged. The baseball player had the counsel of two attorneys and a financial advisor. His wife, a Swedish immigrant, who had been told about the agreement a week before the wedding, had a friend from Sweden advising her. On the day of the wedding, she was told that the wedding would be canceled if she did not sign the agreement. On the way to the Phoenix airport, where they were catching a plane for their wedding in Las Vegas, they stopped at Bonds' lawyer's office and signed an agreement she had seen for the first time only hours before. This agreement dramatically limited the amount of money she would receive upon divorce.

Why did the court declare this prenuptial agreement valid? Because, the judges said, Sun seemed happy, healthy and confident. The week prior Bonds' lawyer had suggested that she retain her own attorney and she chose not to do so. What is more, the wedding was so small and impromptu that Sun could have easily postponed it if she had decided to retain counsel to review the agreement. Other cases in various states have achieved similar results.

The lesson to be learned is that **voluntarily entering into a prenuptial agreement as a consenting adult is entering into a contract you cannot easily walk away from later.**

Today it is also common for the prenuptial agreement to be reviewed after you have been married for several years. Prenuptial agreements can be amended. If, for example, you have children in the course of the marriage, or if one of you becomes seriously ill, or if a significant amount of time has passed, or if there is a change in the tax, estate, or marital laws -- all of these are good reasons to amend your prenuptial agreement.

If you do choose to amend it, then all of the same formalities - separate lawyers, full financial disclosure - apply as much to the amendment as they do to the original agreement. Sometimes the agreement has a built in **"sunset clause"** which specifies that the contract expires if the parties have been married for a certain length of time, which is frequently ten years.

It is important to remember that a prenuptial agreement is the base upon which future planning can be built. In other words, it sets the stage for what each party agrees he or she is entitled to receive.

Strategies for the Re-Married Woman:

1. Discuss the general "terms of the deal" with your fiancé in depth in advance of the drafting of any prenuptial agreement. Let your fiancé know that the agreement is important to you. Be honest in the discussions.

2. Enter into the discussion and negotiation process well in advance of the wedding date and well in advance of the date any invitations to the wedding will be mailed.

3. Hire your own lawyer and suggest that your fiancée do the same. Both parties should have a full understanding of what rights they have and what they are giving up. Make sure that the lawyer you retain has knowledge of this type of agreement.

4. Prepare a detailed financial disclosure: A complete listing of all assets and liabilities, annual earned and unearned income over the past few years, tax returns, financial statements, interests in trusts, family businesses, and potential inheritances.

5. Sign four originals of the prenuptial agreement. Each party should initial the margins of each page, including the financial disclosure pages. Each party should retain one original copy and each attorney should retain an original copy.

CHAPTER NINE

Widowed Woman

"I've had two proposals since I've been a widow. I am a wonderful catch, you know. I have a lot of money."

–RUTH RENDELL

A CLIENT ONCE CALLED ME ON THE VERY DAY HER HUSBAND DIED AND ASKED ME TO GET in touch directly with the Registry of Motor Vehicles because she did not want to lose the ability to keep the low number vanity plates she had on her car. It was early in my career and I did not understand then what I understand now – that her husband had told her to do that in one of the last conversations she'd had with him, and she wanted very badly to follow through on it.

All kinds of emotions run wild right after the death of a loved one - anger, despair, urgency, the need to *do something*. I have come to think of these as fairly common emotional responses to the helplessness a woman feels about her inability to prevent death.

In truth, there is very little that absolutely must be done immediately, and it is important, before taking quick action, to give your emotions time to heal and seek reliable counselors. Above all, don't listen to those who insist that you must "act now, before the opportunity is lost" or who encourage you to do anything that is dramatically different from what you had been doing before. Yes, there are decisions to make, but none should be made hastily. This is not the time to move, sell or buy a house or car, make investments, or think about remarriage.

If you're a new widow, chances are your emotions are raw. The last thing you want to focus on is your finances and your estate plan, and decision-making in this area can be especially difficult for someone accustomed to discussing such issues with a partner, someone who shared your value system and thoughts. It may feel daunting at first to have to make the decisions alone, and planning can involve a lot of difficult decisions. Who should receive your assets? Should you leave your assets to your children? Your grandchildren? Should you leave more assets to one child or one niece or nephew who has been especially good to you?

Some of these larger issues can wait. The first thing you want to do is review your estate planning documents. You probably designated your husband as your health care agent and as your attorney under the durable power of attorney. Now is the time to have those documents revised to put others in charge.

Whom should you choose? Only one person can be named as your health care agent. The reasoning behind that is that when an important decision has to be made, hospitals and health care providers want to be able to turn to one person to make it. With several decision-makers, conflict could arise and the result might be inaction at a time when action could be vital. If you want to select a child as your health care agent and you have more than one child, choose the child (or relative, or friend) who is capable of making tough decisions, like whether or not to terminate life support, and who knows your feelings on the subject and shares them.

If you have several children and want them all to be included, I suggest that you name the child most likely to act in the best way and add a parenthetical after that child's name stating that you are naming that child because he is the oldest or has the most medical background (or whatever the reason) and that you would like that child to consult with all your other children before making any crucial decision. You can also name your children successively.

You can give one person or more than one person the durable power of attorney, but it might be simpler to just name one. If you have two children, for example, and name both and state that they must act together, then obtaining signatures and authority to make decisions may be cumbersome. If you have two children and state in the document that either of them can act, then the document operates as a joint checking account – either child can act without informing the other child. Obviously there are pros and cons to both of these circumstances – a lot of it will depend on trust and control.

Even if your will and trust documents were appropriately drawn up before your spouse died, you will want to review them to be sure that they are updated to cover the distribution of your current assets and that guardians are named for any minor children. Also, in all likelihood the choice of executor should be reviewed. Many of the decisions you and your husband made previously will now seem more real, and this is the time to review them with new scrutiny.

Since the ability to defer estate taxes by passing them to the surviving spouse is now gone, the eventuality of having to pay an estate tax now looms before you, which might make you want to consider gifting, life insurance and other estate planning strategies (depending on your health and age).

Retitling assets is also an important step. Many of your assets may still be in the name of your spouse, naming you as beneficiary. You must change the ownership name on everything from your bank statements and brokerage accounts to motor vehicle registration, deeds, co-ops, wills and all other property. Make your list. Then contact each financial institution where you hold assets. If you have an IRA with Fidelity, for example, you need to obtain a form from Fidelity to change the designation of the beneficiaries. If you prefer, you can hire a bookkeeper, your accountant, or your attorney to assist you with this paperwork.

Along with retitling the assets to your name alone, or to your revocable trust, if you have established one, you also should be thinking about redesignating your beneficiaries for assets, such as life insurance and retirement plan benefits. This is a good time to think through your original choices and see if any revisions should be made. Minors can be the beneficiaries directly, but if you make that designation you should understand that if you die and the minor is under the age of majority, his or her legal guardian will be in charge of the funds. If you feel that the guardian is not the right person to be in charge of the money, you can designate a custodian under the Uniform Transfers to Minors Act. In every state, even if the age of majority is under age 21, the custodian of the account is in charge of the assets until the child reaches age 21. Should you wish to defer distribution past that age, a formal trust document would be required.

Designating the beneficiary of your retirement plans requires special care, since, as far as retirement accounts are concerned, a non-spouse beneficiary must either take out all the money and pay taxes on it in the first five years after your death, or, if you've already started to take out money, the beneficiary must withdraw on the same schedule, as if you were still alive. If you have not started to withdraw funds from a pension, do meet with an accountant or estate planner to determine the best withdrawal election for you and your heirs. Even if withdrawals have begun, there may be ways to stretch the withdrawal period for your heirs.

The rules for designating who should be the beneficiary has to do with income taxes. Retirement accounts are tax-deferred assets, and when you pull them out you accelerate the income taxes. If they are made payable to your estate, then all income taxes on the retirement planning assets must be paid over five years. You can't extend the payments and the income taxes through a child's life expectancy. If you name two children and there is any age spread between them, then the oldest child's life expectancy would be used in determining the income tax consequences and what can be paid out over that child's lifetime.

If you split the IRA into separate accounts naming yourself as the primary owner of each one and giving each account a different beneficiary, then each child's individual life expectancy for income tax purposes will be taken into consideration. Each can also make different investment decisions and can withdraw or accelerate (and pay the income taxes) without affecting the decisions for the other kids.

So, for example, if you have two children, ages 23 and 28, and a $500,000 IRA, you may decide to split it into two $250,000 IRAs and name one child as beneficiary of one IRA and the other the beneficiary of the other. For your purposes it should work the same as if it were one big IRA for payout and income tax consequences. Also, the major financial institutions will price it as if it were one IRA. At your death each child could decide whether to cash it out, leave it in, aggressively invest it, or conservatively invest it - all without the other child's permission.

Dealing with these issues on your own, as a widow, after extreme emotional stress, is difficult. Sometimes widows willingly turn over all decision making to someone else so they won't have to think about these issues. Under the circumstances, this is certainly understandable. However, except in rare instances, no one can deal with most of these issues better than you.

Strategies for the Re-Married Woman:

1. Review your current estate planning documents to determine who is in charge now that your husband is deceased and make appropriate revisions.

2. Review the dispositive provisions of your will and trust to determine who will receive your assets at your death and make sure that it is what you still intend.

3. Coordinate the primary and secondary designation of beneficiary forms of all life insurance policies, IRAs, annuities and pension benefits to make sure they are in order.

4. Fund your revocable trust with the assets you and your husband owned jointly with a right of survivorship or as tenants by the entirety so that at your death those assets will avoid probate.

5. Explore long term care insurance.

6. Get a handle on your revised financial situation and put together a new financial plan that takes these revisions into account. Understand how your pension and social security payments will change after your husband's death. Understand what additional assets you will receive (such as life insurance proceeds). Understand what income sources, such as salary, will be lost. Review your expenses and liabilities to determine how they will be affected.

7. Put together a team of advisors who can assist you in sorting through your husband's affairs and in putting your new financial and estate planning map together.

PART THREE

Focusing on Those You Care About

CHAPTER TEN

Protect Your Children

"Death and taxes and childbirth!
There's never any convenient time for any of them."
–MARGARET MITCHELL

Who should you choose to be your child's guardian?

That, I've found in my 27 years of estate planning, is the most difficult question for couples to agree on and the most common reason they keep revising their estate planning documents.

Factors to consider in selecting guardian(s) include the maturity of the person, whether he or she has a true concern for your children's welfare, and whether he or she has the ability and time to handle the extra responsibilities. What would adding your children to that person's household do to all concerned? Does he or she have children close to the ages of yours? Does he or she share your religious focus, moral beliefs and overall value system? Is he or she willing to take on the responsibility of raising your children?

This is a legal responsibility. The guardian will decide everything from where your children live, what schools they attend, where they worship, and what kind of medical care they get.

My suggestion is to come to as good a decision as you can, knowing that you can always change it. *But make that decision now.* If you put off choosing a guardian and you both die while your children are minors, anyone who is interested can ask the court to be appointed guardian. The judge will then decide - without the benefit of your input - who will do the best job of raising your children. The person the judge chooses may not even be someone on your "short list" of possibilities!

A person or a couple? Do you want to name your sister as your child's guardian or should you name your sister and her husband? There are pros and cons on either side of that decision. If you name just one, the other may harbor resentment and never fully participate in your child's upbringing. On the other hand, if you name both people in the couple to be guardians and they divorce, then your child will be part of that divorce proceeding.

Name **successor guardians,** if at all possible. Your first choice may not be in the right phase of life to act, as a result of divorce, disability, financial hardship or problems with his or her own teenagers, and having successors named makes it easier for everyone.

The Children Decision Tree

PART ONE: Picking a Guardian for Your Young Children

Who should take over parenting responsibilities for your children if you happen to die suddenly? If you don't plan ahead, the government will make the selection for you. This is probably the most emotional decision you will have to make in the estate planning process. The exercises below are designed to help you find the answer.

1) Examining Your Priorities.

The act of parenting involves many different types of activities, responsibilities, value systems, and rituals... so many that we tend to do them instinctively, with little analysis or introspection.

When considering how you want your children to be raised if you are not going to be the one raising them, however, you should take a long hard look at the qualities you want your substitute to bring to the role as parent, and evaluate the relative importance of each of those qualities.

Step One: Examine the guardian characteristics listed below

a) Family – Are blood ties paramount? Do you come from a close-knit family that prides itself on bonding together in times of trouble and "being there" for its own? Do you feel that naming a relative as guardian of your children will keep them in the nest and come closest to duplicating your parenting style? In making this decision, how important is "keeping it in the family"?

b) Finances – You will, as part of your estate planning, take steps to provide your children with enough money, in case you die early, to provide the lifestyle you desire for them. The question is: Does this lifestyle match that of the guardian? Will your children be living as "poor relatives" in a wealthier guardian's home? Or will they be able to enjoy greater material benefits than the guardian's own children, thereby creating tensions? Is the guardian you are choosing financially stable enough to assume this new responsibility?

c) Lifestyle – City life versus country life, staying in the same community versus moving, emphasizing outdoor sports versus emphasizing academics, relaxed supervision versus strict discipline: What are the lifestyle choices you have made in raising your children, and how important is it to you to choose a guardian who will replicate them?

d) Love – They say no one can love you as passionately as your own parents, but some guardians will come closer than others. How important do you feel heartfelt affection is in child rearing, and how important is it to you to choose a guardian you believe will offer your child unconditional love?

e) Religion – If religion has been a backbone of your parenting, can you be sure the guardian you choose will perpetuate the traditions and teachings you have inculcated? Would it bother you if the guardian you choose brings up your children in a different religious faith? How important to you is a religious match in choosing a guardian?

f) Stability – How emotionally stable is the person you are choosing to care for your children? How strong is that person's marriage? Employment record? Position in the community? How good is that person's health? Is age a factor to be considered?

g) Time – How needy for attention are your children and what priority do you want the raising of your children to assume in the guardian's life? IS he/she a workaholic? Overcommitted to community activities? Preoccupied with his/her own problems and responsibilities?

h) Temperament – Is it important to you to have a mood-match in choosing a guardian, and if so, do your children need a soft, loving embrace and an emotionally sensitive attitude, or will it take the personality of a drill sergeant to get them to finish their homework? Do they expect outward shows of affection or cringe at them? Is the person you are considering too moody, irritable or self absorbed to come through?

i) Values – How important are the moral, religious, social, racial and political values you have tried to pass on to your children, and how important is it to you that the guardian you have chosen shares them and will continue the teaching?

STEP TWO: Assign each of the characteristics a number (from 1 to 10), the higher the number the greater that characteristic's importance to you.

CHARACTERISTIC	LEVEL OF IMPORTANCE	prospective guardian #1 _____
Family		
Finances		
Lifestyle		
Love		
Religion		
Stability		
Time		
Temperament		
Values		

STEP THREE: Grade prospective guardians, giving them the points you have allotted for each characteristic they possess, and subtracting the points you have allotted for each characteristic they lack.

prospective guardian #2	prospective guardian #3	prospective guardian #4
_____	_____	_____

2) Evaluating Your Child's Priorities:

Your guardian decision will probably need to be updated as your children grow because their needs vary greatly from one stage of life to another. The nurturing adoration of a grandparent that makes a four-yearold feel loved and secure may suffocate a teenager, for example. At some ages being able to continue living in the same neighborhood with the same friends and going to the same school is more important than living with a beloved aunt and uncle.

Where is your child at this moment?

Step One: Rate the relative importance of the different guardian characteristics, this time examining the characteristics in terms of what you see as *your child's priorities* rather than your own.

Step Two: If you have more than one child, rate each one's priorities separately and compare your results, searching for a compromise.

Part Two: Recording Your Thoughts for Posterity

The overall goal of estate planning is to make sure that you and those you care about are protected in the event that you become disabled or die. In addition to putting your finances in order and taking care of health concerns, you may find yourself searching for an emotional component in estate planning: You may want to leave your thoughts behind as well as your possessions. The following sections discuss the most common formats for doing so, and offer exercises and thought-provoking questions to help you think through some of the issues you might be interested in covering.

Writing a letter to your child's guardian

You will obviously make certain the person you choose as guardian is comfortable with the decision – and with the awesome responsibilities that go with that decision. In addition to holding such discussions, however, many parents choose to write letters to the guardians and trustees they have chosen to care for their children, letters in which they share information and express any concerns they may have about each child's future needs. Such letters are usually placed in sealed envelops with the estate documents, and updated whenever necessary, as situations change. That way the parents know that if they die suddenly, their thoughts will have been recorded, but if they do not, their thoughts will remain private.

Child #1: _____

Child #2: _____

CHARACTERISTIC	CHILD #1'S PRIORITY	CHILD #2'S PRIORITY
Family		
Finances		
Lifestyle		
Love		
Religion		
Stability		
Time		
Temperament		
Values		

An Exercise to Help You Write:

(SUGGESTION: This is an exercise that should be done over time. Read through the questions – choosing the ones that you feel contain the kind of information you are most interested in imparting to your child's guardian - and keep those questions in mind as you go about your normal activities, jotting down different answers as they come to you.)

I: Write each child's name at the top of a column.

A) List below the child's name, all adjectives you would use to describe the child (physically, emotionally, temperamentally, academically, intellectually, in health terms) today.

★Using the adjectives you have written as "helpful guides" write a paragraph describing – explaining - your child.

B) List each child's strengths, as you see them today. Then list each child's weaknesses.

★Using the items you have listed above, write a paragraph describing your greatest concerns about each child, and your hopes, your aspirations for each. What types of supports ? Physical therapy? Psychotherapy? Individual attention? Medical attention? Added nurturing? Discipline? Tutoring? Special education? do you envision each will need to achieve the goals you have for them?

C) List each child's "favorites" - food, activities, friends, sports, relatives, books, movies. Then make a list of the things the child likes least, in the same categories.

★Using the items you have listed above, write a paragraph describing your child's pleasures and displeasures, including suggestions for, perhaps, changing some of those attitudes if you feel change is necessary.

D) When does each child usually wake up? Go to sleep? What meals are eaten as a family? Which are eaten on the run? How much television time per day? How much computer access? How much time with friends? Homework? After school sports? What are the most common family activities? What types of "rituals"- bedtime stories, for example, prayers, parent talks – is each child accustomed to?

★Using the information you have listed above, describe your child's routines, the activities that make up his normal day.

E) [For those with more than one child]: How do your children differ from each other (In personality? In power? In popularity? In self sufficiency? In emotional needs?) What roles do they play in each other's lives? How do they affect each other? How close are they?

★Using the characteristics you have described above, write a paragraph describing the ways the siblings in your family interact and which interactions you feel are beneficial and which are not.

Writing a Letter to Your Child

This may be the most heart-wrenching activity there is – writing a personal letter to be given to (or held for) your child in the event of your sudden death. This is by no means an estate planning necessity. It is, however, something many mothers choose to do ... to ease their children through what would be a profound loss, to impart information they fear will be lost otherwise, or perhaps because they are acutely aware of all the questions that were left unanswered by their own parents' deaths.

(SUGGESTION: It might be easier to write this letter if you view it as a kind of "time capsule" – thoughts recorded at a moment in time. The chance that you will die suddenly is far smaller, after all, than the likelihood that you will live to update this letter in a few years - and then a few years after that – to keep the thoughts current.).

Topics you might want to include:

1) The context: It might help to explain exactly when you are writing this letter, how old your child is, both in terms of age and stage of life, your age and stage of life as well, and your reason for writing the letter.

2) Verification of your child's importance – to you, to others. This may seem silly. Surely he or she knows how you feel! But the validity of memory is often questioned and remembrances do not stand up all that well against the test of time. Studies indicate children who lose parents are constantly searching for proof that they were, in fact, cherished.

3) Information Disclosure: There is a lot of information that only you can impart, and you might want to share this in your letter.

You possess many of the memories that constitute **your child's personal history,** for example. Children young and old love family stories - anecdotes about themselves, their siblings, descriptions of funny family incidents.

You are also probably a key link to **family history,** the person who knows where the relatives are, how they are related, where the ancestors came from, how the family changed from generation to generation. This kind of information is vital to all offspring – young and old as well. Adult children often find themselves left with scrapbooks filled with pictures of people who look like them but whom they cannot identify.

Since science is discovering, increasingly, that genetics plays a key role in physical and mental health, you might want to also discuss **family medical history** here – problems to be on the look out for which have manifested themselves through the generations.

You might also want to share some of your **personal preferences** in the letter. Some women plan their own funerals, for example, leaving instructions for their children to follow regarding the speakers, poetry and music selections and the bible portions they want read. This may sound macabre, but children who want to do "the right thing" when a parent dies often find themselves in a dilemma as to what the "right thing" is. You might want to write out your own obituary as well – and for the same reason. After all, who knows the details and dates of your biography better than you?

Trustees: In addition to appointing guardians to take care of your children you must appoint trustees to manage funds for the children's benefit. My bias is not to name the guardian as the sole trustee. There is too much risk that the lines will blur and the children's funds may be used to pay for more of the household expenses than they should. It could also work the other way. Sometimes if the guardian is the sole trustee, the guardian may not feel comfortable using any of the funds for the increased household expenses, and resentment builds up because the guardian is shouldering more financial responsibility for the increased household expenses than he can or should bear. For those reasons I advise having more than one trustee (with the guardian serving as one, but not the only, trustee). Decisions will come along, such as moving to a larger home. Should your children's funds be part of that? If so, do they ever come back to the children? When will they come back? When the house is sold? When the guardians die? If the guardian has children and they are not able to attend the same schools as your children (because, due to your death, your children have more assets), what happens then? Should the trust funds be used to pay for the tuition of the other children so that resentment does not ensue? The guardian is doing you and your children a real favor by taking the children on and bringing them up. Should the guardian be compensated? If so, by how much? These are the kinds of decisions that the trustees who are in charge of the money will be making. Those decisions should be made with input from the guardian, but there should be checks and balances built into the system.

I recommend that, in addition to the legal documents, each year you write a **memo to the trustees** and put that memo in a sealed envelope that is left with your original documents. In that memo I encourage you to be open about what you see as each child's strengths and weaknesses, what you value, what you wish your children to enjoy, where you feel it is appropriate to spend funds and what things you do not consider it appropriate to spend money on. Everyone has a different sense of what is appropriate for education, for example – public school, private school, boarding school, military school, or parochial school. You cannot assume that others will automatically know your preference. It is your responsibility to provide as much guidance as you can. The guardian and the trustee will feel much more comfortable exerting authority when they know it is in line with what you would have done. Each time you prepare the informal annual memorandum about your child, you may choose to shred the prior year's memo and keep provisions that may no longer be appropriate private and confidential.

How much money is enough? When the children are young, you may want to create wealth through life insurance to make sure that there will be enough, if you die, to clothe, feed, and house them, and assure they will have the educational opportunities you want them to have. In determining the amount of life insurance to put in place many people calculate the cash needs by first estimating any funeral expenses, debts, and unpaid mortgages. Then estimate what would have to be put aside to pay for college. The next step is to calculate how much would be required on an annual basis to cover living expenses for the children, and then to estimate how many years that annual expense would be needed.

If you estimate that the children (and guardian) would need $60,000 per year to maintain their present lifestyle (assuming any mortgage has been paid off and assuming that the college tuition has already been set aside), and that that money would be needed for 20 years, then you would need to have wealth or life insurance in the approximate amount of $1,200,000 to cover those expenses. If you wanted to buffer this by making sure the guardian had an additional sum to do what he or she pleases, then that also should be factored in.

As the children grow past college age, the need to make sure they have enough diminishes, and the question then becomes how much should they have? The issue of needs versus wants becomes more important. How easy do you want to make it for them? How much of a safety net should be provided? What will a significant inheritance do to their lifestyles? Will they buy a bigger car, a second home, quit jobs? What values do you intend to foster with your inheritance? Is your goal to make them richer?

An alternative answer I pose to families who ask that question is, if not your children, then who will receive your assets? The Internal Revenue Service? Charities? These are tough questions to deal with and they are questions on which husband and wife do not always agree.

It is interesting to note that the federal estate tax was not put in place to raise revenue. It was created by President Theodore Roosevelt who felt that if wealth was not diminished from generation to generation, we would end up with an unproductive country. Many of my high net worth clients are coming to that conclusion and making it clear to their children that they will receive a significant amount of wealth but not everything. One wealthy couple I sat down with recently decided to cap the amount each child would receive at $3,000,000 and leave the remaining $30,000,000 of their wealth to a charitable family foundation, which would continue to promote and institute social change in the areas that were important to them. They want all their children (at the death of both parents) to be in charge of that foundation and to make ongoing decisions as to how the funds will be spent.

Special Care for Special Needs. "Special needs children" are those who need extra assistance. They may be disabled, have learning issues, Down Syndrome, Cerebral Palsy, ADD,
autism, muscular dystrophy, depression, obsessive compulsive behavior, closed head injury,
spinal cord injury, or any one of a host of other physical or mental challenges. Sometimes
those problems are severe. Other times children function normally, but at a lower level. Special needs children usually need more emotional support, have higher expenses and need
additional financial resources for a longer time. It is possible a special needs child will require
assistance throughout his or her adult life.

When a special needs child loses his parents (whether that special needs child is 8 years
old or 50 years old), he loses his prime support network. It is important to understand the
devastation of that loss and to try to put a support system in place – just in case – to cushion
the blow. Issues change with age, but in general parents must think through who will moni-
tor that child's welfare, help him apply for and continue to receive benefits, help him decide
whether to continue working, how to get around, and fulfill supplemental needs like vacations or travel. Special care must be given to who the guardian, trustee and advocate will be,
and it is especially important in this case to line up successors.

Many special needs children and adults pay for food, shelter and some medical costs
with money from governmental programs funded by the Social Security Administration and
Medicaid and some state sponsored programs. Even if a child is covered under a private
health insurance plan, however, that may not be enough. Medicare and private insurance do
not cover residential care or most medication expenses. Medicaid *does* cover those expenses
and for most special needs children Medicaid is the most important government benefit.
Special needs trusts which preserve **Medicaid eligibility** can be created to allow the child
to be eligible for governmental assistance. The special needs child/beneficiary should not
have the right to demand funds from the trust as that demand right jeopardizes Medicaid
eligibility.

Some children's "special needs" are not grave enough to require governmental assistance.
And then there are others whose problems are not serious enough….. but perhaps may be
if they deteriorate. The issue that must be decided is whether the special needs trust should
be one that qualifies for governmental assistance (and is therefore is more restrictive) or one
that is more conventional – one, for example, that simply provides for the child's health and
support for his or her lifetime.

Keeping the child's assets in trust reduces the risk that the inheritance will be squandered,
mismanaged or subject to creditor claims. Early in my career, a father and daughter came to
my office so that the father could do estate planning. His wife had died and the daughter
was his only child. She was in her late 30s, a college graduate who had only held lower level

jobs because of her problems. She had been hospitalized several times in the past as a non functioning manic depressive, but she was now taking her medication regularly and had not had a setback for more than ten years.

The father and daughter had several open discussions with me about what to do with the father's assets. The daughter pleaded with her father, insisting that she was fine, that she was on medication, that she knew enough to take it, that she had saved $100,000 on her own, and that she did not want her assets to be controlled by anyone else when her father died.

Her father's compromise was to put the assets in a trust but agree that if, at the end of five years, the daughter thought she could serve as co-trustee, she was entitled to do so. He died a few years later. The daughter was so bereft at his death that she stopped taking her medication and was involuntarily committed to a state hospital for a month. When she got out, she had no other friends and fell under the influence of a family who took her in, mixed up her medication, and, once the five years passed, repeatedly brought her to the bank to withdraw funds from the trust. They spent her entire inheritance on themselves and kicked her out when she had nothing left. Ultimately they were prosecuted and some money was recovered.

In his passionate desire to believe that his daughter would be all right, that father underestimated the stabilizing effect he'd had on her life.

Dividing Assets Fairly: If you do have a special needs child or a child who is not disabled or on governmental assistance but who has greater needs than the other children, the question of how to divide the assets can be very tricky. Some parents prefer to have all assets held in a special needs trust for the child who needs them, and then at that child's death have the trust end and the money distributed among the other children.

Other parents do not feel that the special needs child (because of the government programs available) will actually need all that much money and do not feel right denying their other children an inheritance. If need be, they feel, the other children will take care of the special needs child. This approach, of course, comes with risks. It's possible the other children may predecease the special needs child, spend the money on their own legitimate needs, become disabled or get divorced and need the funds.

For that reason sometimes **a special needs trust will be funded with life insurance** – and the special needs child will be omitted from the other terms of the estate plan. That way, if the trust is irrevocable (and funded only with life insurance) when the insurance is paid, it will come in free of gift, estate and income taxes. To the extent the special needs child needs it, it is there. To the extent it is not needed, it will eventually be distributed to the other children free of any tax consequence.

One of the most difficult issues for a special needs child is where the child will live if the parents die. Frequently that child cannot live by himself. Yet it is a tremendous burden to a sibling or family member to take in that child. For that reason I have seen an increasing trend of parents placing special needs children in group homes during their lifetimes so that a support structure has been put in place and the adjustment that comes with the death of parent (and best friend) does not also mean a change in home.

It is especially important when planning for the future of a special needs child that the assets are coordinated with the plan. All beneficiaries of life insurance policies, pension plans, IRAs, and annuities must be reviewed. If a special needs child is named directly (instead of the trust) or if there is no designation of beneficiary and the asset defaults through your estate, then your plan can quickly unravel and the receipt of those funds by the disabled child will jeopardize his government eligibility.

Stepchildren: With the rise of nontraditional families in this country children no longer mean primarily children born of the marriage of two parents who keep living together. Stepchildren provide interesting issues in that, unless legally adopted, a step-child does not have the legal right to inherit your assets. You must make provisions in your will, trust or by the designation of assets in order for your stepchildren to receive an inheritance.

In the "yours, mine and ours" families, who will receive what when both parents dies is sometimes easier to decide than if only one person in the couple has children and those children have another parent. In my experience much depends on how old the step-children were when brought into the new marriage, what the comparative wealth has been and what the relationship is between the stepchildren and step parent. I have had step parents refuse to include stepchildren in their plans because the stepchildren have been rude and uncooperative with them, and they have felt no need to benefit them. I have had step parents give sometimes nominal, sometimes significant sums to the step children to show that they mattered. I have had step parents include step children as if they were their own children. I have seen step parents treat different step children differently – giving more to those with whom they'd had a closer relationship and less to others. These are tough waters to navigate, and consideration should be given to the consequences of these decisions. When a decision is reached, it is important that the plans for husband and wife are coordinated. If, for example, you are married and have children from a prior marriage and you die first, leaving all of your assets to your husband outright, and his will does not include your children, then your children will be disinherited by both of you. Many parents in subsequent marriages choose to leave assets to their children at their death even if the spouse survives. That provides assurance that no matter what the spouse does or who the spouse subsequently marries, those children will be provided for. A good vehicle for this is **additional life insurance** because that does not make the surviving spouse feel that it came out of the wealth they acquired together. (If life insurance is the vehicle it should be owned in an irrevocable insurance trust so that it is insulated from estate taxes).

Another wrinkle in the traditional family is those children born to gay partnerships or marriages. If you are the parent or grandparent in that situation you may be concerned as to the legal consequences. In most states, that child can inherit as a natural or adopted child of the parent, but not from the same sex spouse. In some states a married same sex couple can go through a second parent adoption and in some states that will then be recognized for inheritance purposes. If the child or grandchild is not the natural or adopted child and you want that child or grandchild to receive assets in the estate plan, then it is important say so specifically in your estate planning documents and in the designation of beneficiary forms for your retirement plans and annuities.

Strategies to Protect your Children:

1. Have you executed a will naming a guardian for your minor children?

2. Have you named a successor guardian?

3. Have you given thought to who will manage the money your children inherit – A custodian under the Uniform Transfers to Minors Act? A trustee? Are you designating a person or a team of people/institutions? Have you lined up successors?

4. Have you thought through the reasons that money should be expended to the children? For education? For post graduation education? To buy a car? For a wedding? Down payment on a house?

5. Have you calculated your assets and income to make sure that if you die before your children are educated, are there are sufficient funds to pay for their living expenses and college tuition?

6. If there aren't sufficient funds, have you met with your advisors and considered the appropriate amount of life insurance?

7. Have you left a memorandum or letter to the guardians and trustees explaining what you would like to see happen if you are unable to be there to watch your children grow up?

8. Have you given thought to what the guardian should receive financially (compensation, reimbursement of expenses, funds to care for the enlarged household?)

9. Have you coordinated the primary and secondary beneficiaries of all life insurance policies, annuities and retirement plan assets to be sure that the assets are put in the hands of those who will be in charge of your children's money (custodians under a Uniform Transfers to Minors Act or trust for their benefit), rather than having those assets payable outright to children at a very young age?

10. Have you given thought to distribution ages – at what age or ages your children should have the right to overrule the trustee and withdraw funds regardless of what the trustee thinks is appropriate?

CHAPTER ELEVEN

Protect your Husband

"We can't cross a bridge until we come to it;
but I always like to lay down a pontoon ahead of time."
–BERNARD BARUCH

MARRIED COUPLES EMBARK ON ESTATE PLANNING TO MAKE SURE THAT THE SURVIVING spouse has sufficient income, that the assets are distributed as they wish, and that the smallest amount of taxes are due when they both die. A good way to prepare for this task is to think through what you would like your husband to receive outright at your death, what should be given directly to your children, and whether there are others who need to be taken care of.

Most of us grew up expecting our husbands to take care of us, and that frequently happens. But it is also our obligation to protect our husbands. That means evaluating your individual circumstances carefully to determine what type of protection is necessary. If your husband is in a high risk business in which he could be sued and lose his net worth, for example, such as obstetrician or surgeon, it is possible that you own most of the family assets as protection.

Should you predecease him, should those assets be given back to him or should they be added to a trust that he is the beneficiary of during his lifetime so that he is protected from creditors even after your death? If he doesn't own many of the family assets, how does that lead to minimizing the overall estate taxes your children will have to pay?

Caroline and her physician husband, Tom, came to me with just those questions. Even though he had never been sued for malpractice, Tom knew too many other physicians who had been, and as long as he lived he did not want to own any significant assets in his name. He knew that by putting all of the family assets in Caroline's name, his major creditor risk was Caroline: that if she ever wanted to divorce him, she would already own their entire net worth. But he was not worried about that. He told me they had been married for 25 years, had gone through a lot together, and he doubted that would ever happen. It was a risk he was willing to run.

I mentioned that if he predeceased Caroline there were not enough assets in his name to shelter the current federal and state estate tax exemption amount from his taxable estate. He had a significant retirement planning asset, but, as I explained to him, that asset was not a good candidate to be payable to a trust, since doing so would undercut Caroline's ability to "roll over" that asset for income tax purposes and defer paying any income taxes on it until she was at the age when she would be forced to withdraw it.

The power of untaxed income growing in that retirement planning asset was significant, and since their primary goal was to protect each other, sacrificing that income tax goal to make sure that eventually the children had the benefit of his utilizing that credit if he predeceased Caroline just did not make sense.

After a lengthy discussion he decided, for now, to purchase a $5,000,000 life insurance policy on his life and make it payable to his trust. If he predeceased Caroline, that money would go in there, create $5,000,000 of additional wealth, provide her with supplemental income (approximately $250,000 in annual income) and produce an asset that would pass to the children free of tax when they both died.

If he survived her, he told me he would drop the life insurance, as at that point his other assets would count toward the exclusion. If he retired and they decided to shift assets from her name to his, since that would also qualify for his unified credit, he would drop the insurance then too.

With that decided, we discussed Caroline's predeceasing him. If she did so and all of the assets were paid outright to him, they would not qualify to be used for her federal and state estate tax exemption amounts, and, in addition, she would be handing it over to the wolves. If he owned those assets himself, they would be easy prey if he ever *did* have creditor problems. For that reason we came up with a plan where all of her assets (including both the family home and the vacation home) did not pass to Tom by her will, but instead were transferred to a trust he was a co-beneficiary of (along with their children) during his lifetime. Because of the future creditor issues, I recommended that Tom not be the sole trustee of that trust. We decided that a major financial institution they were both comfortable with should serve that role if the time came. We also agreed that the trust document would provide that Tom would have the right (after Caroline's death) once every three years to remove and replace that financial institution serving as trustee with another independent financial institution. He does not have to exercise that right – it is there as a precaution.

There would not have to be any reason to make that change; however he was limited to once every three years. That would give him flexibility and some control to determine which financial institution would be best, at different moments in life, to navigate the family's finances, and, at the same time it would prevent anyone from thinking he was managing from the sidelines and manipulating who was in control.

It is important to know that there was no current creditor or lawsuit threatening from the wings when the planning and the discussion took place. There was just a general feeling that someday something like that could occur.

If there had been a specific creditor or a specific lawsuit when he transferred the assets to Caroline, the plan would probably not have held up. In every state in this country there is a law that protects the creditors if you convey assets out of your name to avoid them. (Certain assets are exempt from the reach of your creditors; in most states exempt assets include some or all of the equity in your home). It should also be noted that if you want to do this and you live in a community property state you must sign an agreement by which the property in your name is declared separate property. Without that, even if it is in your name it will be available for his debts.

Are you concerned that if you predecease your husband there will be no one there if he becomes disabled or incapacitated to make sure that his needs are met? If you are not there, will he have the financial wherewithal to pay for caregivers? Should long term care insurance be put in place now? What is his medical history? What is his family's medical history?

Are you concerned that if he remarries and he has all of the assets outright he will leave them to a new spouse and not your children? What if he later gets divorced? Will the assets the two of you built together be put at risk? Have you discussed that with him and come to agreeable terms as to how to resolve those issues?

Mandy loved her husband a great deal. Her husband was very successful at work and very dependent on her for all aspects of their personal life – organizing, traveling, running errands, cooking, making sure the house was in order. She was absolutely sure that if she predeceased him, he would remarry in a year, just because he would not be able to be alone. With three young children she was concerned about how to make sure her husband was protected, and also make sure that if she predeceased him, her children would be the ultimate beneficiary of what she and her husband had accumulated together. This was all very much on her mind because she had just lost a dear friend to breast cancer and was feeling her own mortality. Her goal was to first obtain an initial understanding of what the possibilities were for this type of plan, then to bring her husband into the office for a joint meeting so together they could get a plan implemented.

I explained to her that any asset in her name would be under her control. Any asset in her husband's name would be under his control, and any asset they owned jointly or which was payable to the spouse, would be under the survivor's control.

She did not have enough assets in her name to fully utilize her federal and state tax exemption amounts, and so, by moving more of the joint assets into her name alone she would be able to accomplish two goals. She could fully utilize her credit so that if she predeceased her husband, when the estate taxes did hit, they would pay the least amount of taxes. And she could also create a trust of which her husband and children would be the beneficiaries during his lifetime, but stipulate that if he remarried, he could receive no further benefits from her trust unless an independent trustee (such as professional trustee, advisor or financial institution) thought it was appropriate for him to receive the funds. This would protect the funds for her children's eventual use in the event of a divorce from his second wife.

Assets that are used to fund the applicable exclusion amount can be restricted against subsequent remarriage. Assets that are in excess of that cannot carry that restriction without jeopardizing the tax-free-to-spouse status, because the Internal Revenue Code mandates that putting such a restriction on use would jeopardize the unlimited amount that can pass to the spouse tax free.

I also explained to Mandy that if she followed that plan her federal and state estate tax exemption amounts would be as safe as it could be if she predeceased he husband, and if she felt that more should be locked in for the kids, she could purchase a life insurance policy on her life and have it owned by and payable to an irrevocable trust that her husband and children were permissible beneficiaries of, again with an independent trustee who could determine what level of assets would be distributed to him if he remarried.

Since the insurance trust would be excluded from both their taxable estates, there would be no prohibition on limiting the funds available to her husband if he remarried. She thought these were helpful suggestions. I made it clear to her that when they both came in I would make these thoughts known to him too and she should be prepared to live and die by the sword - that he may want exactly the same provisions in his plan for her. She was comfortable with that and went home to discuss this with him in greater detail. They both incorporated these provisions in their plans, and he transferred enough assets to her to fully utilize her unified credit.

Are you a prime income earner? If you die before your husband and your income evaporates, can he support his lifestyle? Can he continue to support the family and educate the children? Should there be life insurance on your life to protect against those risks? If the face amount of the life insurance is significant and would make the estate taxable it should probably be held in an irrevocable insurance trust.

What if you are widowed later in life, never thought you would ever be happy again, but then met someone, married, and now feel a need to make sure he is protected? Milly, a 70 year old widow came to me with just that question. She met Tony, 82 years old, a widower with no children, at a church bingo party. They really hit it off, enjoyed long walks and dinners together. After a few years they married. He sold his modest house and moved into her house. Her children thought he was wonderful and were delighted he was in Milly's life, yet Milly was not sure how they would feel if she put a provision in her will that Tony be permitted to live in her home (the home where she and her deceased husband had raised their children) after her death.

Tony was not worried. He told her he would move out and live on his firefighter's pension. Milly did not think that was fair. After all, he had sold his house and was spending a lot of the assets on the two of them now. She was caught between both worlds. She decided to specify in her estate plan that, at her death, the house be put in a trust with an independent trustee. Tony would be able to live there after her death. She mandated in the trust that as long as he lived there he was responsible to pay the real estate taxes, homeowners insurance and ordinary repairs. She felt confident in his ability to do that from his pension. When he moved out or at his death the trustee would be directed to sell the house and distribute the proceeds to the children. If he moved out during his lifetime, when the house was sold, the independent trustee was given the authority to distribute to him (if the trustee thought it was appropriate) enough money to relocate, money to cover the cost of moving, first and last months rent, etc.

Another soon-to-be married couple in their later years, Sam and Anna, came to me to ask about long term care. Both had had spouses die of long term illnesses and neither of them wanted to put the other through that again. They were past the age where they thought long term care insurance was a financially viable alternative. I explained to them that spouses (whether married three days or thirty years) were obligated to support each other and that it would be against public policy to override that with a contract. The most that could be drafted into a contract is that if either of them had long term care needs (at home assistance or more extreme), that spouse's income and assets must be used before the healthy spouse's income and assets were depleted. I mentioned that the only absolute way to protect assets was to live together and not marry (assuming it was not a common law marriage state).

They did not feel comfortable doing that – both were practicing Catholics. So we took a look at current living arrangements. It made sense to put them in a living situation where if one of them needed assistance, the resources were there for help. They were both mobile enough to be accepted at an assisted living facility and they made a joint decision to sell their homes and to move into a unit that provided those services and allowed a transfer to a nursing home if a need for that occurred.

These are some of the issues to consider when thinking about protecting your husband.

Many of the concepts discussed in other chapters of this book apply here too and should be considered as part of the overall planning process.

There are no federal estate taxes on transfers (lifetime or death time) between spouses as long as the spouses are United States citizens. For federal estate tax purposes ,if you are married to a non-United States citizen, then special rules and special trusts apply to make sure that the least amount of estate taxes are paid if you predecease your husband and that the least amount of estate taxes are due when you both die. (This is unlike if you are married to a United States citizen in which case the Internal Revenue Code will allow the deferral of the taxes until both of you die).

In some states, you are considered married even if you are not legally married. These are "common law states" and include Alabama, Colorado, District of Columbia, Georgia (if you started living together before 1/1/97), Idaho (if you started living together before 1/1/96), Iowa, Kansas, Montana, New Hampshire (for inheritance purposes only), Ohio (if you started living together before 10/10/91), Oklahoma, Pennsylvania, Rhode Island, South Carolina, Texas and Utah.

In these common law states, in order to be considered "married," however, in addition to having lived together for a significant period of time you must also have held yourself out as a married couple and intend to eventually be married. Holding yourself out as a married couple can be evidenced by filing joint income tax returns or by calling each other spouse, husband or wife. If you enter into common law marriage you are considered married for inheritance purposes. If you enter into a common law marriage in one state and move to another state, as long as the common law marriage was valid under the laws of the state in which you were married you are considered married in the non-common law marriage state, because the full faith and credit clause of the United States Constitution compels the recognition of a valid marriage made under the laws of a sister state.

If you are in a common law marriage, even though you have the right to inherit if your husband dies (and vice versa), the practical reality is that you may have to prove that marriage was valid prior to receiving the inheritance, and other family members may launch an attack. Living together without a common law marriage gives the partner no legal standing in most states.

If you are married and live in a community property state the rules are different. For the most part, all you earn during your marriage and any property you acquire during your marriage with those earnings are considered community property and therefore equally owned by husbands and wives. The same goes for debt. All debts incurred during marriage are the couple's debts. If you are married in a community property state, then one-half of your community property goes to your husband at death unless your will says otherwise. You can dispose of your separate property (which includes property you owned prior to marriage, property given just to you and, property you inherit) to anyone you want.

Community property states include Arizona, California, Idaho, Louisiana, Nevada, New Mexico, Texas, Washington and Wisconsin. In Alaska if you sign an agreement, certain assets are community property assets. You and your husband can override the community property rules by a written agreement that turns community property into separate property or separate property into community property.

An advantage to living in a community property state is that if you hold property jointly, at the death of the first spouse the income tax basis in the entire property is stepped up, meaning the asset can be sold for that value without incurring a capital gains tax. (If you live in a non community property state then only one-half of that joint asset – the half that you received at your husband's death, would receive that stepped up basis). Should you cross state lines, live in a community property state, such as California, buy a house (community property asset) and then sell it and move to a non community property state such as Massachusetts where you buy a new home, make sure you have the deed drafted to reflect that you intend that the home remain community property so that at the death of the first spouse the surviving spouse receives the full stepped up income tax basis.

If you do not live in a community property state, then there is no rule that property acquired during the marriage belongs to both people. Still, in almost every state a surviving spouse cannot be cut out of a spouse's estate plan completely.

Over the years I have had people who wanted to cut out or reduce their spouse's rights to inheritance for all kinds of reasons. For example, in a second marriage without a prenuptial agreement and they wanted to leave most of their assets to their children from a prior marriage rather to than their current spouse, or because they were worried a spouse's creditors would take all, or because they were on the verge of divorce, and thus didn't want to hand over any more assets than they had to.

In most states even if you omit your husband from your estate plan, he has the right to claim one-fourth to one-half of your assets at your death – no matter what your estate plan provides. However, in most states the spouse has to go to court to claim that right. If he does, it cannot be disputed, but if he doesn't, then the claim expires and your estate plan will be honored.

Strategies to Protect Your Husband:

1. Know what assets are in your name, what assets are in your husband's name, and what assets are held jointly.

2. Know who the primary and secondary beneficiaries are of any life insurance policy on your life and your husband's life.

3. Know who the primary and secondary beneficiaries are of any retirement plans, IRAs, 401(k)s or annuities are and know who the primary and secondary beneficiaries are of any of your husband's retirement plans, IRAs, 401(k)s or annuities are.

4. Know what your household assets are and what your household income is.

5. Be sure you and your husband have durable powers of attorney, health care proxies, wills and trusts.

6. Know who is named Executor in both of your estate planning documents, and who is named Trustee.

7. Know what your husband's income will be if you become disabled and your salary does not continue to be paid to support the family. If appropriate explore the purchase of disability insurance.

8. Know what your husband will receive if you predecease him whether he will receive those assets outright or in trust, what debt exists and how it will be paid, and what liquid assets will be available to pay bills, debts, and mortgages.

9. Know what your husband's income will be if you predecease him and your income is no longer available, and how your husband will be able to educate your children.

10. Make sure your husband knows who the family advisors are (lawyer, accountant, financial planner, life insurance professional, investment advisor, business advisor) and to whom to turn if he needs assistance.

11. Explore the purchase of long term care insurance for you and your husband.

12. Designate a guardian and a trustee for your minor children in the event of your and your husband's deaths, and decide at what age your children should receive funds.

13. Review your property and casualty insurance to make sure that the appropriate levels of insurance are in place and consider purchasing umbrella liability coverage.

CHAPTER TWELVE

Protect Your Elderly Parents

"If I'd known I was gonna live this long, I'd have taken beter care of myself.."
–EUBIE BLAKE ON REACHING 100

MORE THAN ONE QUARTER OF FAMILY MEMBERS IN THE UNITED STATES TODAY ARE involved in some way in the care of their elderly parents. Taking steps to prepare for your parents' future needs is not only important for your parents. It is important for you.

The first step is to find out what preparations have already been made. Have they filled out a **health proxy** and a **power of attorney?** Do they have **long term health insurance?** What legal documents have they signed, and where are the documents located? Have they thought through how they want to be taken care of, if and when they need care, and who will take care of them? When were the documents executed and are they current? Do they need to be updated? What kind of **health coverage** will they have? Will they have enough money to cover costs?

The sooner such questions are asked, the better. It is very important to discuss estate planning with your parents while they are both mentally and physically healthy. If they wait to make arrangements until after one of them is incapacitated in some way, their options will be seriously limited.

That said, I'm the first to admit a discussion about estate planning is never easy, because it involves two discussion topics that are both personal and discomforting for most people: money and death. Discussing the subject with your parents also involves role reversal. And then there is the added possibility that your efforts could be seen as privacy invasion or greed, since you will probably be one of the beneficiaries of the plan. All these aspects can make estate planning discussions with parents especially difficult.

I urge clients to be as sensitive as possible. It often helps to start by explaining that your main goal is to make sure their wishes are followed and to do so, you need to know exactly what those wishes are, and what they would want you to do if an emergency or tragedy strikes.

Another approach I have seen work is to discuss your own financial situation with them. That's often a catalyst for your parents to start opening up about their estate plans. They may be just as eager to discuss their estate planning as you are, but they may not know where or how to begin.

All too often adult children procrastinate until the situation becomes critical and choices are limited. Cindy, a 61 year old woman came to me after five years of watching her elderly mother slip mentally. Like all too many of us, Cindy had maintained a state of denial, blaming the lack of memory and understanding on other factors. She decided her mother was not active enough to keep her mind alert that she was just slowing down, that she had reached a stage where she no longer cared about details that did not affect her personally. It was only when it became clear that her mother's condition was beyond normal forgetfulness that Cindy was forced to deal with it, and by the time she did, her mother had become fearful, suspicious and confused.

Cindy was spending increasing time caring for her mother - bringing her to the doctor, assisting with her bathing, dressing and eating – and Cindy had a full time job. She began to explore social services that might help. She enrolled her mother with **Meals on Wheels** and had **visiting nurses** check in on her twice a day. She found a terrific **adult day care** program for her mother, all of which seemed, for a year, to make things better.

But as her mother's health continued to deteriorate, Cindy's work was suffering and so was her family, and Cindy herself was becoming more and more stressed out. Some days her mother did not even know who Cindy was. It was killing Cindy to watch someone who had been fiercely independent all her life lose the ability to take care of herself. Watching her mother's steady decline was, Cindy told me, "the long goodbye." She had come to the decision that she was going to do something she thought she would never do – put her mother in a nursing home.

Her mother did not have **long term care insurance,** and Cindy deeply regretted not having discussed the possibility of getting it with her mother long ago. The subject of long term care insurance is a tough one, I told her, and probably by the time she was ready to bring it up with her mother, her mother was no longer eligible to purchase it.

Her mother's assets were: the family home, now worth about $500,000, two certificates of deposit worth about $150,000, and a social security income of about $1300 per month.

Could **Medicare** help?

I explained to Cindy that Medicare pays the doctor and hospital bills for people who are disabled and over the age of 65. Medicare also pays 100 of the cost for the first 20 days of a stay in a Medicare approved rehab facility. However, Medicare does *not* pay for custodial care or nursing home care, and that was what her mother needed, not medical care. She needed assistance with what is known as the **activities of daily living (ADLs).** These include getting out of bed, moving around the house, bathing, dressing, eating and using the toilet.

Medicare was never meant to cover all the health care expenses of an elderly person. There are other gaps it does not cover. Unfortunately, her mother had never purchased any of the **"gap coverage"** - the private insurance policies that can be purchased by persons who are over age 65 and most times provide for prescription medication, short term home care or short term stays in skilled nursing facilities.

We discussed the option of **Medicaid,** the federal/state program that provides medical aid for people whose income is below a set level. Many elderly Americans either spend or transfer assets to bring their income down to the point where the government pays for the cost of their care. Medicaid pays for almost half of the nation's nursing home costs. Approximately ten of Medicaid patients enter a nursing home as a private, paying patient only to spend so much on their nursing care that in the end they become eligible for Medicaid. In most states Medicaid does not pay for home care.

Cindy was opposed to the idea of transferring assets in order to qualify for Medicaid. She felt as long as her mother had assets of her own, her own money should be used for her care. With the average annual cost of a nursing home exceeding $80,000 per year and the average annual cost of at home care exceeding $50,000 range, Cindy knew that her mother's care would deplete her assets. She was comfortable with the decision.

We then discussed how to find out which facilities were the best for the dementia level her mother had. It was clear that, since her mother was no longer capable of carrying out the "ADLs" - activities of daily living - on her own, she had passed the stage for **assisted living** – the type of seniors-only residential facility that usually provides meals, assistance with personal care and housekeeping and keeps an eye on the resident's health and safety. Nor was she able to remain independent enough to be a candidate for a **continuing care retirement community** – a facility that provides a continuum of care – independent living, assisted living, and some skilled nursing care as well. Cindy knew her mother had passed all of those points.

I suggested that she hire a **geriatric care manager** - a social worker, counselor, nurse, or gerontologist who specializes in assisting older people and their families find the right kind of care for their circumstances. Her mother's physician put her in touch with a geriatric care manager and Cindy placed her mother in a nursing home facility.

Long Term Care Insurance. Sally had a very active 76 year old father who lived in a senior citizens complex in Florida. His good friend and neighbor had deteriorated in the past year and, since the neighbor had purchased long term care insurance in advance, she was able to get the care that she needed daily from caregivers who came to her home. What is more, she was not paying one penny for that care.

Sally called me because, even though her father was in good shape, she wanted to understand more about long term care insurance. She knew that her father, a fiercely independent man, would want to remain in his own home as long as he could, and, since he and her mother had worked hard to accumulate and maintain their assets, they would not want all their money to be depleted by a lingering illness. She felt it would be awkward for her, as a daughter, to have to tend to his physical needs in declining years and even if he moved in with her and her family, having the ability to have independent caregivers handle aspects of his personal care would be very appealing.

I explained to her that **long term care insurance** protects someone from catastrophic long term care expenses. Many older people who are not in perfect health (who is expected to be after age 40?) qualify for coverage as long as they aren't *already* afflicted with the types of illnesses that will definitely require long term care, illnesses like Parkinson's disease, Alzheimer's, dementia, multiple sclerosis, osteoporosis (if it has resulted in fractures), muscular dystrophy, diabetes, and ALS.

Some long term care policies pay a set amount of money for each day a patient is confined in a facility or receives care in the home. Others reimburse the holder up to a certain amount for care received. (It is interesting to note that caregiver children are not eligible to be paid from this type of policy for any care given the parent). The amount of care the policy pays for and the length of time the policy covers care expenses varies from policy to policy. Obviously, premiums are higher for policies that provide higher amounts of daily coverage for longer periods of time.

Long term care is offered through group policies, through employers or associations such as A.A.R.P. and through individual policies. Most policies have a deductible or elimination period, which means the policy begins to pay after the person has been in the facility or has been cared for at home for a certain number of days.

I told Sally that her father's financial resources should be taken into consideration when

---

Legalese Defined
Reverse Mortgage: A loan that enables an owner to borrow against the equity in his/her residence in either a lump sum or periodic payments and defers the repayment of the loan until either the residence is sold or the owner dies.

deciding whether or not to purchase long term care. If between his income and his investments he could support having someone come in and care for him or pay for a nursing home himself then it may not make sense to purchase the policy. That's because long term care insurance can be expensive (though the cost of long term care can also be expensive). The cost of staying in a nursing home today is staggering, and at-home care is not much cheaper.

Sally decided that even though her father might be able to finance it on his own, she felt strongly that long term care insurance would be a better option. She said her father had always been very conservative with his spending and she didn't want to fight with him about whether or not he was ready to pay to have someone come in to assist him. She felt that if the insurance was there, it would be easier to get him to have someone care for him. She also told me she and her husband felt so strongly about her father's getting long term care insurance that they were willing to pay for the cost of the premium now.

I told her that some states offer income tax deductions or credits if you pay long term care premiums. If Sally and her husband chose to pay for her dad's long term care insurance premiums they would be making sure that there were available funds for his care and they could also view the premium payments as an investment that would protect their ultimate inheritance of his assets. I also suggested to Sally that in a few years she and her husband explore the purchase of long term care insurance for their own needs. When the long term care insurance policy is purchased by someone in their 50s or 60s it is possible to find a policy that offers ten or twenty year payment options that would allow you to finish paying for coverage by the time you reach age 65 or retire. Another option for Sally (and probably not for her dad) would be to explore a special type of long term care policy that is linked to a life insurance policy and provides a death benefit to survivors if the premium payments were not used for long term care.

Reverse Mortgages. Home equity is the single biggest financial asset many senior citizens have. About 80 of Americans 62 and older own their homes, and most of them own their houses free and clear – without any mortgage to pay off. Reverse mortgages are special types of loans that enable people 62 and over to convert the equity they have in their homes into cash while they continue to live at home for as long as they want. (Yes, you can keep your home and get what it's worth at the same time!)

Jane, an 83 year old widow in fair physical condition, with no children lived in a modest home in the suburbs and was using her own money to pay for a caretaker to live with her and make sure she was fine. She called me frantically one day when she realized she only had $40,000 in assets left, and she did not, under any circumstances, want to leave her home.

She thought she might deed her home over to the caretaker in exchange for an agreement that the caretaker would care for her for the rest of her life.

I told her I did not think that was a good idea. What if the caretaker predeceased her? What if the caretaker herself became disabled? In addition, Jane was paying the caretaker (who was not a rich woman) wages. What would the two of them do for grocery money once Jane's last $40,000 ran out?

"OK," Jane told me, "then come up with another way I can achieve my main objective, which is to stay in my own home until I die."

Since Jane owned her house she was an ideal candidate for a **reverse mortgage,** a loan based on the amount of money her home was worth which Jane could use to pay for her living expenses and health care needs. I explained to her that payments from a reverse mortgage can be in the form of a single lump sum of cash, regular monthly advances or a line of credit. Setting it up as a line of credit would give her a personal account she could draw against, up to the value of the house. The terms of reverse mortgages vary, although almost all provide a guarantee of life tenancy.

I explained to Jane that if she sold her home or permanently moved out of the house (or at her death) the mortgage would become due, which means it would be important for her to understand the lender's rules on how long she would be allowed to stay out of her home – whether for a trip (which although unlikely is always possible) or an extended nursing home stay (which she adamantly told me would never happen).

She also would need to explore when the term of the mortgage would end and she would not be able to receive any more money. There will be a time when the cash flow ends even though the note may not yet be due. The total amount that is owed under a reverse mortgage can not be more than the value of the property. If the house was sold, after the mortgage was paid off, she would receive the balance of the proceeds. After taking out a reverse mortgage she would still be the owner of the home and, as such, would still be responsible for maintaining the property, paying the property taxes and keeping it insured.

I also explained to Jane that the amount of money she could get depended on three factors: her age (in most cases the older the borrower is, the more money that can be loaned), the equity in the home (and since Jane did not have a mortgage on the home currently that would work in her favor), and the loan costs. Some reverse mortgages are insured, which adds to the cost of borrowing but guarantees receipt of the payments.

I explained to Jane that most people who consider this option prefer the line of credit type of payment, and that not all credit lines offered as reverse mortgages are the same. It is really important to explore the differences. There are three types of reverse mortgage loans – those offered by the Federally Insured **Home Equity Conversion Mortgage** (HECM) which is administered by the Federal Housing Administration and offered by banks, mortgage companies and other private sector lenders, **proprietary reverse mortgages** (backed by private

118

companies), and **public sector loans** (offered by local and state governments for a specific purpose such as to repair or improve a house or pay property taxes). The federal HECM program usually has the lowest cost loans.

Jane liked the idea of a reverse mortgage and eventually went through with it. The reverse mortgage provided her with enough money to pay for her care at home until her death.

Strategies for Caring for Your Elderly Parents:

1. Make sure they have signed a Health Care Proxy and a Durable Power of Attorney and that those documents have been revised since 1996 to include the privacy provisions which pertain to HIPPA.

2. Have a family discussion about care long before it is necessary to act. Explore the role the family will play. Will they want to stay at home? Move in with family members? Enter a residential facility? Discuss who will be the primary caregiver. Discuss who will be sharing in the caregiving responsibilities.

3. Assess your parent's finances and their own ability to pay for care. Obtain a listing of their assets, liabilities, and income (including Social Security payments, other retirement income and the account name and numbers into which they are deposited).

4. Evaluate your parent's medical and personal needs.

5. Know who the doctor is and how to contact him or her. Determine if a geriatric assessment is necessary. Find out what medications are currently being taken, dosage and side effects.

6. Find competent medical and geriatric care givers.

7. Review medical coverage, prescription plans, Medicare, Medigap, Medicaid options.

8. Explore the purchase of long term care policies.

CHAPTER THIRTEEN

Protect Your Significant Other

*"I don't want to achieve immortality through my work.
I want to achieve it by not dying"*
–WOODY ALLEN

MARILYN AND TED WERE LIVING TOGETHER, SURE ABOUT THEIR FEELINGS FOR EACH OTHER, but also fairly certain they would never marry. After going through a horrific divorce and custody battle with his first wife, Ted had vowed he'd never again put himself in a position where the court would be able to interfere with his life. He loved Marilyn but had told her from the beginning that any kind of legal marriage was out of the question.

When they came to me for estate planning, they had been together ten years – accumulating assets together and sharing a household - and their life was good. I explained to them that one of the first concerns they should address is what would happen if one of them became very sick or disabled. Unmarried couples do not automatically have legal standing to make health care or financial decisions for each other. If you become ill or incapacitated and have not executed a **health care proxy** giving your partner the authority to make decisions about your medical treatment, then the law in virtually every state will authorize your heirs at law or next of kin to handle those decisions for you. In Ted's case the decision maker would be his 22-year-old daughter, who was on cordial terms with Marilyn but on better terms with her own mother.

Marilyn was aghast at this. She made it clear to Ted that she would include his daughter in any decision, but she felt strongly that she should have the final say. Ted agreed, and health care proxies were signed.

Only a few states give unmarried partners the right to make medical decisions – but even in those states biological family members are given priority too, so to avoid confusion and conflict it is best to make your desires known through a health care proxy.

When the discussion turned to finances, the same issues of next of kin and heirs at law having priority over unmarried partners arose. Marilyn and Ted signed **durable power of attorney** agreements, each giving the other the power to handle all financial affairs.

Since Marilyn and Ted were not married, they could not take advantage of the **unlimited marital deduction,** the unlimited amount of money that could pass free of gift and estate taxes from one spouse to another. They were, of course, still entitled to leave each other the $5,000,000 current **federal applicable exclusion** amount. Although their assets were under the federal estate tax threshold they exceeded the state estate tax exemption thresholds and for state estate tax purposes, their assets were just hitting the borderline between what was nontaxable and what would be taxable. Marilyn and Ted were concerned that if their assets continued appreciating and they remained unmarried, a state estate tax would be due when the first one of them died.

They discussed buying life insurance to make it easier for them to pay that tax, and, in addition, to enable Ted to leave his daughter assets even if Marilyn survived him. They decided to buy a $500,000 life insurance policy on Ted's life and put it in **an irrevocable life insurance trust** (i.e. owned by a "trust," and therefore removed from Ted's estate, and administered by a "trustee" who would follow Ted's instructions as to how the money was to be used) and name his daughter as the only beneficiary of that policy. That way, whether Ted died before or after Marilyn, his daughter would receive those funds taxfree.

A decision was also made to name a professional financial institution as the trustee of that trust, as Marilyn did not want to be in the position of deciding how much money his daughter should or should not receive, and Ted did not want his ex-wife to have any say at all in that decision.

They also decided to take out life insurance policies on each other, so that each would each receive $500,000 at the other's death. They would "cross own" the policies —Marilyn would be the owner and primary beneficiary of the policy on Ted's life and Ted would be the owner and primary beneficiary of the policy on Marilyn's life. That way if Marilyn were to predecease Ted, the only assets in her taxable estate would be those in which she had an ownership interest. Since Ted would be the owner and the primary beneficiary of the life insurance (not Marilyn or her estate) then Ted would collect the $500,000, and there would be no gift, income, or estate tax to pay.

Legalese Defined
"Living together" agreement: An agreement, usually between persons who are not married but living together, which sets forth their respective rights to assets and income should the relationship terminate.

Of course, after Ted collects the money it will be included in his later taxable estate, but they did not think it was worth restricting the funds in trust to remove it from both taxable estates. Their primary goal was to make sure that the other person received the assets tax free and without restriction. What happened to the proceeds at the death of both of them, and the eventual tax consequences, were not of concern.

I also mentioned that since they now owned their home together, they might wish to consider entering into **a "living together" agreement,** which is similar to a prenuptial agreement, only for unmarried partners. They could set forth now, while they were getting along, who would get what in the event that they ended their relationship. Without that agreement, if the relationship ended and they were unable to come to conclusion as to the division of assets, the courts would be involved – Ted's worst nightmare.

A living together agreement could also set up a process for the way disputes would be resolved, such as mediation rather than a court fight, if the relationship ended. Since most people feel "their home is their castle" – and are quite emotional about it - an agreement that covers the house should also include other factors, such as who gets what back if the house is sold. If, for example, Marilyn made the full down payment, an agreement could stipulate that she should be repaid before the balance of the equity is split. If Ted is paying a disproportionate share of the mortgage and expenses, that can also be taken into account.

How the title to the house is held is also important. Should it be passed on to the survivor if one of them dies, and therefore held as a right of survivorship? Or would they prefer that, at the death of the first partner, that person's interest in the house passes through his or her will? If so, then title to the house is held jointly as **tenants in common,** a form of joint ownership that does not include a survivorship right.

I asked if one of them wanted, for business reasons, for example, to be able to stay in the house if the relationship ended or the other partner died. Should we set up a right of first refusal for that person, the right to be given the first option to buy if the property went up for sale? If so, how will the house be valued? All of these are areas of concern that can be addressed in a living together agreement.

Then we talked about wills. In most states unmarried partners have no legal right to the deceased partner's assets. In a few states - California, Hawaii, Massachusetts and Vermont - if domestic partners are registered, then there may be an automatic right to inherit, but the laws in those states are new and untested, so it's foolish to rely on them.

Establishing a will (and, if appropriate, a trust) which makes clear what you intend to leave to whom and who should be in charge is thus even more important for unmarried partners than for married partners. In most states unmarried partners do not have legal standing, and do not even have to be notified of the administration of the deceased partner's estate.

Since Marilyn and Ted can't qualify for an **unlimited marital deduction,** I suggested they think about **lifetime transfers, and gifts.** I explained that each person has the right to gift $13,000 per year to anyone else, pay anyone's tuition or medical expenses (as long as it is paid directly to the provider) and, in addition, has the once in a lifetime $5,000,000 applicable exclusion amount. They could use those options, if they wanted, to shift assets into each other's name to even out their estates or lower an estate that would be taxed at death. Other than gifts in those parameters, however, transfers between the unmarried partners may be subject to the federal gift tax.

For federal estate tax purposes, even if property is owned jointly by unmarried partners, and the ownership avoids probate at the death of the first partner, that does not mean that it avoids estate tax. When property is co-owned by people other than spouses it is included in the decedent's federal taxable estate, except to the extent it can be shown that the surviving partner either originally owned the asset or contributed to it.

Following along on the taxes, since the partners are not married, if their combined estates exceed the applicable exclusion amount, there is the real risk that the assets will be taxed twice – once when they pass from one partner to the other (to the extent the amount exceeds the applicable exclusion amount) and again in the surviving partner's estate (to the extent the applicable exclusion amount is exceeded again). Of course, this assumes that the surviving partner did not have to deplete those funds during his or her lifetime.

For that reason, when unmarried partners wish to benefit the same people eventually and care about what estate taxes are paid when both die, they might want to establish **living trusts** and have the primary beneficiary be the surviving partner, but restrict the surviving partner's access to the funds enough to keep it out of the surviving partner's estate. In other words, the assets will be taxed once – between both estates, not twice.

Avoiding probate is often a goal for unmarried partners because it enables them to keep their financial affairs private. Since avoiding a court procedure means there is no legal requirement to notify the heirs at law about the administration of the estate, no one has to know how much money you had or what was left to you. In a probate proceeding the next of kin are notified (whether or not they are the beneficiaries under the will) and given a right to object. Assets that are owned jointly with a right of survivorship, paid to a person by designation of contract (such as a life insurance policy, IRA or annuity) or assets that were put in trust during lifetime generally avoid probate.

Many times I've had unmarried partners (usually of the same sex) tell me that they were concerned that when a partner died his or her family would "come out of the woodwork" and challenge the estate to claim benefits. In those occasions it is very important to avoid probate. It may also be advisable to include what is now known as a "Sinatra" clause, after

Frank Sinatra who included one in his will. The **Sinatra clause** specifies that anyone who challenges the provisions of the will, any trust that the decedent established or the administration of the estate forfeits any benefits that person would have otherwise received. Frequently, a will or trust will mandate that a bequest will be given to a child and if the child is not living then to that child's children. When the Sinatra clause is included I think it is important to also make sure that the challenging child beneficiary and his children are excluded too. Otherwise the child beneficiary may launch a fight, be dropped from the benefits list because of the Sinatra clause, only to have his children receive the benefits (getting in "the back door").

I have also decided – from years of experience – that if a decision is made to employ the Sinatra clause, it's a good idea to leave the person who is going to be disinherited something that they consider worthwhile so that the decision to fight or not to fight is made after deliberation –not because of spite. If there is something you can offer that the person would regret losing, they will usually think twice before starting a fight.

It is also very important for unmarried couples to coordinate the designation of beneficiary forms for retirement plans, annuities, and IRAs. If you intend to leave any of those assets to an unmarried partner you must do so specifically, since in virtually every state the unmarried partner has no automatic right to those assets.

Some states now legally recognize same-sex marriages. That means same-sex couples will be subject to the same *state laws* as married heterosexual couples for child custody, alimony and divorce. Current *federal law,* however, does not recognize same sex marriage. For that reason there is no unlimited marital deduction for transfers of assets between same-sex spouses. Thus, the same principles discussed above for Marilyn and Ted apply to same sex marriages for federal tax purposes, and, unless they reside in a state that recognizes same sex marriage, for state tax purposes as well.

Strategies for Unmarried Partners:

1. Have you executed a health care proxy? Is a successor named?

2. Have you executed a durable power of attorney? Is a successor named?

3. Have you thought about drafting a "living together" agreement?

4. Have you made your funeral and burial instructions clear?

5. Have you executed a will? And, if appropriate, a living trust?

6. Have you reviewed with your advisors the tax consequences of leaving your assets to your partner? Have you reviewed with your advisors the tax consequences of your receipt of assets your partner intends to leave you?

7. Have you explored long term care insurance?

8. Do you know what assets you will be able to access if your significant other becomes disabled or incapacitated?

9. What about your debt – have you both reviewed how that will be handled at the first death?

CHAPTER FOURTEEN

Protect your Charity

"As you grow older you will discover that you have two hands, one for helping yourself and the other for helping others."
–AUDREY HEPBURN

ACCORDING TO *BUSINESSWEEK* MAGAZINE, BILL AND MELINDA GATES ARE THE MOST generous donors in America, having given away over $23 billion, more than half of their net worth. Warren Buffet, the founders of Intel, the founders of Dell Computers, Ted Turner, Mayor Michael Bloomberg, Oprah Winfrey and Sanford Weill and the founder of FaceBook are all heavy givers too. Now you may say: "Easy for them. They can afford it! They can give away a fortune and still have more than enough money to do whatever they want for their rest of their lives and to be sure that their children and grandchildren and great-grandchildren are protected."

However, you can have much, much, much less than Bill and Melinda Gates, but still have enough in assets to have to pay estate taxes when you die. The question for you is: Would you rather give that excess to the charity of your choice, or donate it to the Internal Revenue Service or your state taxing authority?

Giving to reduce the amount of taxes you have to pay is, of course, only one of the reasons to make a charitable gift. There are plenty of others. And the other reasons are important to remember as the estate tax reasons to donate to charity (the rising estate tax exemption and the lower effective estate tax marginal rate) diminish. Women, I find, in particular want to be agents for change. When they give to a charity, they tend to retain a personal interest in what happens with the money. Women can be very creative in thinking about what the problem is they are most concerned about, and then putting their money toward solving it. Many of the great institutions – the Girl Scouts, American Red Cross, Smith College, Mount Holyoke College - were started by women with a philanthropic vision.

Making a gift to a charitable organization now, during your lifetime, will enable you to help those causes you deem worthy, while you reduce your taxable estate, and, in some cases, earn an income tax deduction as well. Of course, before you make the gift, you should be sure that giving up the assetwill not affect the way you live the rest of your life: that you do not, in fact, *need* that asset for yourself or for your family.

There are many types of charitable giving vehicles to consider: charitable bequests, life insurance, gift annuities, pooled income funds, charitable remainder trusts, charitable lead trusts, donor advised funds, and private foundations.

Charitable Bequests: A charitable bequest is a direct gift (during your lifetime or at your death) to a charitable organization. Many annual gifts to charities are tax motivated. A very common year-end gift is to transfer an asset that has greatly appreciated in value – stock or real estate - to a charity directly in order to receive an immediate tax deduction for the value of the donated stock at the time you gift it. This enables you to avoid paying a capital gains tax on the amount that the stock has appreciated.

Charitable gifts don't have to be financial assets.   Some people give artwork or collections of personal items. Others give books and manuscripts. Many of my clients have chosen to leave a specific dollar amount at death to a charitable organization they feel aligned with – a school, museum or hospital. Such gifts can be for specific purposes – such as a scholarship fund - or they can be given for the charity to use any way they wish.

One client of mine wanted to make sure that her favorite museum received $1,000,000 at her death, but she did not want to take $1,000,000 of her assets away from her children and leave it to the charity. Instead she decided to take out a life insurance policy on herself that would be owned by and payable to the museum at her death. The annual premium was $10,000, and she told the museum that each year she would donate $10,000 to it with the understanding that when the museum received the $10,000, it would use the money to pay the life insurance premium. She was very comfortable knowing that at her death the museum would receive the $1,000,000, and the $10,000 the premium cost was within her budget.

Charitable Remainder Trusts: If you have an asset that is significant in value and has a hefty built-in capital gain, it may be too significant an asset for you to give up completely. Rather than donating it outright to a charity, you may wish to *retain the income from the sale of that asset...* and to do so without having to pay a capital gains tax. So, instead you donate this substantially appreciated asset such as stock or piece of real estate to a special type of trust known as a *charitable remainder trust*. Once the asset is transferred to the trust, it is irrevocable. You will never be able to get the principal back, but you, or you and your spouse, or you and your spouse and your children (your choice which) can be the life beneficiaries. When the last of the persons specified as "beneficiaries" dies, the balance will be distributed to charities you either choose now or name in your will.

When the trustee of the charitable remainder trust sells the asset, since the ultimate beneficiary of the trust is a charity, there is no capital gains tax and that means the payout to you from the investments is greater than it would have been if you had sold the asset, paid the tax on the gain, and invested the difference. If you cannot afford to give up access to that principal, this type of technique is not for you. However, it works beautifully if there is a portion of your assets that you envision only being used during your lifetime for income.

Using a charitable remainder trust makes sense for someone who can afford to give up the property put in trust, but wants the increased cash flow during his lifetime that would be enhanced from avoiding the capital gains tax and re-investing some of the trust assets. It can be used for many different reasons. A client of mine in his 80s, for example, had an extremely valuable musical instrument that had been passed down from generation to generation. None of his children knew how to play it, and he was very concerned that if he died no one would be able to make sure it had a safe home, and no one would know how to capture its value. No matter how much he loved owning it, he felt it was his responsibility to take control of its sale. If he sold it for the $1,000,000 he anticipated it was worth, he would be incurring a major capital gain. He did not feel that he needed the principal to live on, and so he decided to contribute the instrument to a **charitable remainder trust.** The trustee of the trust negotiated with a premier world auction house and sold the instrument for even more than my client had expected.

Another client of mine had three cousins who owned the family business. They decided it was time to sell the operating business – which had been in their family for many years - and decided to explore the possibility of transferring the stock to charitable remainder trusts to avoid the capital gain. Two of the three cousins did just that, but the third wanted to keep control of the principal and use it for future real estate deals, and did not go the way of the charitable trust.

Every client of mine who has decided to go this route has had charitable inclinations and philanthropic intent. No one should ever decide to give away access to principal unless they are sure they will not need it, and no one should ever do so just to reduce their taxes. (The tax tail should never wag the dog!) It is just one of the factors to consider when planning.

There are other, more complicated charitable trusts that are undertaken by people of significant wealth. A **charitable lead trust,** for example, is an irrevocable trust from which charitable organizations receive the income for a designated time period and the donor gets an income tax deduction for transferring his assets into the trust. When the asset is transferred to a charity, the capital gain is avoided. When the time period is up, whatever remains in the trust is distributed to the family as specified by the donor, either in trust or outright.

The key difference between the charitable remainder trust and the charitable lead trust is that with the charitable lead trust the bequests to the charities go first or *lead*. During your lifetime (or for a certain term of years) the charities, and not the family members, receive the annual payout. At your death or at the end of the term, your family will receive what is left. The value of what passes ultimately to your family members is considered a taxable gift as determined by actuarial tables published by the Internal Revenue Service. Even so, this kind of a technique is leveraged and can ultimately put a great deal more wealth into family hands.

And then there are **private charitable foundations,** trusts or corporations established and funded entirely with the private money of a wealthy family. The M.S. Hershey Foundation that owns the controlling interest of Hershey chocolate is a private foundation. Milton Hershey and his wife did not have any children, and so, at his death (after hers), he placed his entire fortune into a private foundation whose mission is to support orphan boys. It is a very significant, and because of it, there is now a very good school in Hershey, Pennsylvania that educates orphan boys at no cost at all.

For clients with more modest annual charitable gift concerns who do not want to pay a lawyer to draft a trust or an accountant to file the annual income tax returns, I often recommend setting up a **donor advised fund at a major financial institution or community foundation.** You can get a tax deduction for a gift in any amount, and "donor advised" means the institution or foundation will put your money in whichever of its charities you prefer. "Community foundations" are local organizations that give money to charities in their jurisdiction. These appeal to donors who don't have a specific charity in mind, but would like to help those in their area.

Pooled income funds, gift annuities and deferred gift annuities are other alternatives. They are usually offered by hospitals, colleges, and community programs. Since they are also often administered by those charitable entities, the costs are borne by the entity, not by you. **A pooled income fund** allows you to give away assets, yet still retain the dividends they generate during your lifetime. All the individual donor contributions to the pooled income fund are put together and managed professionally. Each donor receives a return on her investment in proportion to the investment's age of the total pool. For example if you contribute $1,000 to a pooled income fund that has total assets of $100,000 your age of the fund's assets is one percent and your share of the interest and dividends the funds receives will be one percent. When you and your surviving beneficiary die (if you have named one) then the charity will receive the remaining principal.

A charitable gift annuity gives you another flexible way to sell an asset without incurring a capital gain and receive some cash back from the investment for your lifetime (or the lifetime of a subsequent beneficiary, if you so desire). In a turbulent economy in which many individuals are concerned about what their income is and want certainty so that they can budget, this tool has become increasingly popular. If, for example, you have a favorite charity such as your local hospital and you own stock worth $10,000 dollars that has a hefty capital gains tax built in and is not producing much income, you can transfer your stock to the hospital by a signed agreement. You will receive back fixed payments that will not vary in amount; that amount is initially set by your age and other factors. The gift is irrevocable; you will never be able to receive the principal back and for that reason you will receive an income tax deduction. Also, part of what you receive back will be tax free. That asset will, of course, be removed from your gross estate and at your death the balance will go to the charity you chose.

Strategies for Charitable Gifting:

1. For lifetime gifting consider what assets you have that have a current low income tax basis - stock, artwork, antiques, and real estate.

2. Consider whether you would like to unlock the value of those assets by selling them now, avoiding the capital gains tax and converting them to an income flow for your lifetime. Make sure that you consider that you will be giving up the principal asset value during your lifetime.

3. Think about which charities you wish to benefit; and think about whether they should receive the assets at once or over a period of time.

4. Discuss the various charitable gifting strategies with your estate planning and tax advisors.

5. Consider making strategic charitable gifts of more significance at your death, or if you are married when both of you die.

PART FOUR

Estate Planning is an Ever-Evolving Process

CHAPTER FIFTEEN

Sam and Sue, a Case Study

"Would you tell me which way I ought to go from here?" asked Alice.
"That depends a good deal on where you want to get," said the Cat.
"I really don't care where" replied Alice.
"Then it doesn't much matter which way you go," said the Cat.
– LEWIS CARROLL, ALICE'S ADVENTURES IN WONDERLAND (1865)

At age 35

When they first approached me for advice on estate planning, Sam and Sue were college-educated 35- year-olds with two small children. They had decided Sue would be an "at home Mom" while the children were young. Sam had a solid salary - $70,000 a year and rising.

Their most important goal, at this stage, was to name guardians for their children, but they were having problems deciding who would be the best choice. Sam's brother, Christopher, was levelheaded, shared their religious background and income level, and had children around the age of theirs. But Christopher's marriage was on shaky ground and Sam and Sue did not want their children to be involved in the fallout of a divorce.

Sue's sister Margaret and her husband Tom, on the other hand, lived nearby and had a strong marriage, but a smaller house than Sam and Sue and a smaller income. Sam and Sue feared that adding their children to Margaret's household would be too much of a burden.

As we talked, I explained that this is the choice that is the most difficult for young parents to make, and it is important to realize that the decision is not written in stone. It can be changed at any subsequent point by a one paragraph amendment.

I also asked them to consider another dimension: Whether they wanted to name a person or a couple as guardian. If, for example, they named Christopher alone and he did get divorced, then his wife would have no legal standing in raising Sam and Sue's children. But if they named Christopher alone, and he stayed married, and his wife assisted in raising their children but did not have the legal authority to make decisions, she might very well become resentful. This could put additional pressure both on their marriage and on her feelings for Sam and Sue's children.

In addition to the guardian decision, I urged them to make some financial provisions - buying life insurance, for example, so that if something happened to them their children would be well provided for. I also pointed out that they could name Margaret and Tom guardians for their children and assure that Margaret and Tom had the resources to do so by making provisions in their wills and trusts that would allow the funds to be used both for their own children and for the guardian's children.

We looked at life insurance policies as a means of providing for the family in the event of either Sam or Sue's. How much would be needed? Enough to pay off the home mortgage, and to replace Sam's salary if he predeceased Sue, and enough to pay for child care if Sue predeceased Sam. (The Social Security Administration does pay a monthly stipend to minor children of a deceased parent who has paid into the system but it is not enough to support that child in full).

At this stage, while Sam was young and healthy and thus easily insurable - and because the family was totally dependent upon his income - I suggested they explore **disability insurance** as well – insurance that would pay the family if Sam had an injury, car accident, or other illness that prevented him from being employed at his current salary level. (Life insurance pays out only at death, but disability insurance could provide an income flow to the family throughout his lifetime.)

Sam said his company offered disability insurance as part of the executive package. I suggested he supplement the company's offering with another policy, because jobs rarely last forever and disability insurance is usually not portable. If Sam left his present employer, he might not be able to take the disability policy with him, and by that time he would be older with health issues that might preclude him from obtaining the right coverage.

Estate planning goes hand in hand with financial planning, and a coordinated plan should cover lifetime expenses as well. Even though their children were just toddlers, we also talked about starting to put money away for college tuition.

We also discussed the **estate planning documents they would need - durable powers of attorney, health care proxies, wills, and trusts.** These documents form the foundation of all future estate planning.

The **durable power of attorney** enables each spouse to give the other the legal authority to sign his or her name in handling the couple's financial affairs, so that if one of them becomes disabled or incapacitated but lives, the other spouse can continue to write checks, make bank deposits, and sell assets. Sam and Sue own their home jointly, with a right of survivorship. That means if one of them dies, the other will automatically receive the house. If they do not have durable powers of attorney in place and instead of dying, one of them is in a major car accident and lives, then even though the house is in both their names, it would be frozen and the healthy spouse would not be able to sell it or mortgage it without court approval.

Just because you are legally married doesn't mean a spouse has the authority to act for you in legal or financial matters.

A health care proxy is a document in which each spouse gives the other the authority to make medical care decisions if she or he becomes unable to make them. This runs from the routine (access to medical records and medication) to the more serious (deciding when and if life support should be terminated). Under federal law only one person at a time can be named as health care agent, but a health care proxy can name a succession of people as alternatives. This is done so that someone else can take over if Sam and Sue are in the same car crash, and neither one of them is in a condition to make medical decisions. A copy of the health care proxy is given to the primary care physician and becomes part of the medical record.

The will is a document that comes into operation at death and disposes of the couple's assets in accordance with their instructions. **Trusts** are legal documents, or contracts. At this stage in Sam and Sue's life, the trust would be a **revocable trust** – one that could be changed or amended during their lifetimes. Children under the age of 18 – or 21 in some states – are considered too young to manage their assets themselves, and so trustees are appointed to handle the money for them and pay the child or the guardian for the health, education, support or maintenance. Without a trust the longest that assets can be held for the benefit of a minor beneficiary is age 21. With a trust the assets can be held until the child reaches any specified age. The primary purpose of the trusts at Sam and Sue's young age is to make sure that if both of them died, their assets would be managed for their children in a way that made sense.

At Age 42:

When Sam and Sue returned seven years later, both children were in school all day long, and Sue was back at work on a part time basis. They both felt it was important for Sue to be home in the morning when the children went off to school and in the afternoon when they returned. Sue's income - $25,000 – gave the family some breathing room in terms of extra financial needs, like furniture or a new car, and also allowed them to increase their annual savings.

Their children were older and distinct personalities were starting to emerge. Their 11-year-old son, John was a focused kid and a good student. At 10, his younger brother, Tim, had been diagnosed with a learning disability and was becoming a discipline problem in school. A special tutor had been hired, but thus far did not seem to be helping much. They worried about Tim's future needs.

I suggested that as part of the estate planning process they might want to write a letter to the trustees and guardians every year that explained their concerns about each child. They put such a letter in a sealed envelope with the estate planning documents, and seemed relieved by the knowledge that if something happened to them, their recent thoughts would have been recorded, but at the same time, if they did not die, those thoughts would remain private.

Sam had left the company he had been working for and gone into business with Tony, one of his former co-workers, and the two were doing very well financially. Tony had a wife and children too. Sam and Tony were concerned about what would happen to the business if something happened to either of them. Neither wanted the other man's spouse involved in the business, but on the other hand, each of them wanted to make sure that if he died his wife and family would be provided for.

I suggested an agreement known as **a cross purchase or buyout agreement** – a contract with Tony, backed up with life insurance policies, that specified that if either Sam or Tony died, the surviving partner would be obligated to collect the life insurance and buy out the deceased partner's share of the business. Sam saw this as an effective means of protecting each other, the business and their families.

To make the surviving partner's life easier when running the business, I suggested that Sam and Tony, in addition to putting the life insurance in place for buyout purposes, also buy what is known as **key man insurance,** taking out a $250,000 policy on each of their lives that would be owned by and payable to the company. This would provide both a cushion of cash to take care of any emergency and fund a salary for the replacement of the deceased partner.

We reviewed the legal documents they had put in place seven years earlier to see if any of them needed to be revised. Since their combined salaries had increased, they decided to increase their life insurance, to be sure they had adequate replacement money in the event of either one's death.

Sam and Sue also explored **saving funds for their own retirement.** Their current expenses were high and they wanted to make sure they were saving enough for college tuition, but they were also worried that if they didn't start saving soon, they wouldn't have enough when they retired. Sam decided, on his accountant's advice, to deduct contributions to a retirement plan from his company's taxable income, since those assets, when they begin to fund the plan, can grow on an income tax deferred basis until the funds are needed for retirement. We discussed Sam having Sue work a few days a week for him so they could also fund a retirement plan for her.

At Age 49

When Sam and Sue were 49 years old, their children were approaching college age, and the need for any sort of guardian was dissipating. Other concerns, however, were cropping up. They reviewed their estate planning documents and decided that 35 - the age they had previously determined their sons could receive the funds of the estate – was too young. They amended the documents, specifying that each child could withdraw one half of his share of the estate at age 35 and the balance at age 40.

The children of friends of theirs had just gotten divorced. What if one of their sons married someone who later divorced him and took with her half of the inheritance Sam and Sue had worked so hard to create? They wanted their estate planning documents revised to include the proviso that all gifts/inheritances they gave to their children remained in their blood line.

Their son, John had expressed interest in working in Sam's business long term, but it was too early to tell if he really wanted to, so instead of planning for the succession of the business at this point, they decided to keep things the way they were: that if Sam died Tony would buy out his share. However, they made a note that in five or ten years they might want to revise that and instead of having Sam's share be bought out by Tony, have Sam's share pass on to John.

They also made a note to consider making special provisions for their younger son, Tim, at a future date. Despite private tutoring and counseling, Tim at age 17 was barely passing his subjects, feeling increasingly alienated from his peers, and acting out both at home and at school. They were not sure Tim would be able to graduate from high school, and saw little chance of his going to college… but were still hopeful that maturity might change things.

Sam and Sue had enough savings and enough confidence in Sam's increased cash flow that they decided to buy a second home – one on the water an hour and a half away. Their plan was to spend weekends there in the spring. They made a significant down payment on the second home and took out a mortgage, comforted by the knowledge that if things got tight, they could cover both the mortgage and the real estate taxes by renting out the house for the first few summers. Their accountant told them that by owning the house for investment reasons and using it for personal pleasure at a very minimum level they could depreciate the building over a period of time, which would significantly reduce their income taxes. He warned them that depreciating the house would have a negative consequence if they sold it, since the income taxes would have to be partially recaptured. That did not bother them, since they hoped the house would stay in the family for a long time.

Sam parents, Martin and Joan, were in their early 70s and having some health problems. As a result Sam and Sue were feeling a great deal of pressure from all of life's competing interests – work, the children's needs, and the medical care of their parents.

Sam's father had been diagnosed as having incipient senile dementia. Sam and Sue had begun to investigate how the disease might progress and what precautions they should consider making. They started to put a plan in place to give Joan respite care and began to look into alternative programs, such as adult day care.

They understood that it was important for Sam's parents to put their own affairs in order – making sure that Sam and Sue had the legal authority to handle their financial affairs if they became disabled or incapacitated and also to make medical care decisions if Joan and Martin were no longer able to do so on their own.

At Age 56

During this visit Sam and Sue were most concerned about their younger son, Tim. He was 23 now, still having behavioral problems, working at low paying jobs, and unable to stay employed for more than a few months at a time. Where would he live if something happened to them? How would he support himself? They did not want his older brother John to have to dedicate his life to Tim's care.

We put a support structure in place so that other people who understood Tim's issues would be able to protect him if he were not able to do so himself, but made the strucutre flexible enough to permit those people to give Tim more freedom if he became able to handle increased responsibility.

They made John one of the trustees who would be in charge of the money for Tim but made sure he was not the only one. They wanted there to be three trustees, ruling by majority vote so that Tim and John could remain close, and John could honestly say that it was up to the other people who served with him when tough decisions had to be made.

They also decided that when both of them died, the house was not to be distributed to either of their sons but instead would become an asset of the trust for Tim's benefit as long as he wanted to live there. Making sure he had a roof over his head for the rest of his life was a very important goal. They decided that the best way to do that was to keep the house in the trust and make the board of trustees responsible for its care and upkeep – making sure the real estate taxes were paid, and that regular maintenance occurred.

They stipulated in the trust document that the trustees had the authority to sell the house with Tim's approval and reinvest the proceeds in another home or condominium that he could live in, and that others could live in the house with him. They also made provisions that the trustees could retain whatever advisors they needed for Tim's benefit – social workers, mental health professionals, tutors, career counselors, etc.

John, at age 24, was dating several different women, working very hard in the family business but also considering graduate school. Sam thought it was only right that John be able to share in the appreciation of the business's value and asked me what I thought about giving John shares of stock in the family business. I told him it was a good idea from an overall estate planning point of view, since gifts to John of the stock over time would reduce Sam and Sue's taxable estate and would also remove the appreciation on the gifted stock. There was, however, one potential problem: once the shares of stock were in John's name, they would be considered his asset and when he married, his assets could (depending on the state he was living in) become marital property. In other words, if they gifted John 15 of the company, and John's wife chose to divorce him, the 15 could be divided in a divorce, and his wife would have the right to have the entire company appraised as part of the divorce proceeding.

I told Sam one way he could give John the stock and still protect his business would be to ask John to execute **a prenuptial agreement** with his future bride.

At first they did not like that idea, considering it "unromantic," but the more we talked about all of the situations that they were seeing and that I have seen, the more positive they became about designing a prenuptial agreement that mandated that any assets that were gifted to John or Tim by Sue, Sam or other family members would remain each son's separate property. On the other hand, any income or assets acquired or earned during the sons' marriages would not be covered by the prenuptial agreement and would be negotiated and split during any divorce proceeding.

This protected the family business from any future divorce proceeding, but at the same time allowed Sam and Sue to begin to gift it to John.

We also discussed the value of telling John and Tim about the prenuptial agreement now. That way, I explained, when they met someone they wanted to marry, it would not be a sudden personal decision, but rather something that had long been part of the family's rules.

Sam asked me what would happen if one of his sons refused to bring up the agreement or if his future daughter-in-law refused to sign it. I told him that very rarely had I seen anyone refuse to sign this type of prenuptial agreement. If that happened, however, Sam and Sue always had the option of revising their own estate planning documents so that the trusts were more restrictive and assets were not left outright to their son but instead maintained in trust under the control of trustees. Since the son could not access those assets without the permission of the trustee, it would be difficult to include them as marital assets in a divorce.

I also explained that I did not like this choice as well as I did the prenuptial agreement as it is very controlling and restricts the son's access to the funds for his entire lifetime.

Sam and Sue decided to mention the pre-nuptial agreement to their sons now.

Sam's parents' continuing health problems had convinced both Sam and Sue to take steps to make sure they protected each other and their children from this kind of burden in the future. We looked over **long term care insurance policies** – policies that pay for the increased cost of custodial care. I suggested they choose a policy that includes an "a**t home rider**" – a provision that allows the healthy spouse to use the insurance money to pay for someone to help out at home with custodial care. Also, since Sam had these types of issues in his family but none had evidenced in Sue's family, I suggested they might want to buy more long term care insurance for Sam than for Sue.

Since their net worth has continued to appreciate we embarked on more in depth estate tax planning during this session, to make sure that the estate taxes that may be due when both of them die were reduced to the largest extent possible.

In Their Later Years

That is as far as Sam and Sue have come in updating their estate planning. They understand that they are not done planning. Revisions will be made as their lives evolve. The changes we make during future sessions will, obviously, depend upon the changes in their lives and lifestyle.

We might give more serious attention to succession planning in Sam's business, for example. As he and his partner age, they should start thinking about who will take over if they either die or want to retire. Does Sam's son, John want to carry on? Provisions could be put in place for either the two partners' children, outsiders, or current employees to gradually assume responsibility.

If Tim's lifetime outlook does not improve, they will probably update the permanent trust they have set up for their son, putting in place a succession of trustees to make sure someone will always be available during his lifetime to make sure he is all right.

If, say, Sam dies and Sue remarries, Sue might want to sign a prenuptial agreement with her new spouse to specify that her assets go to her children at her death and his go to his children. Since once you marry, you are obligated to support your spouse, a prenuptial agreement could also protect those assets for the next generation by specifying that if either one of them needed custodial care, that person's assets would be fully depleted before the healthy spouse's assets were touched. Another common clause, when one spouse in a new marriage like this moves into the home of the other, is to specify that if one predeceases the other, the children of the deceased will give surviving spouse the right to live in the house rent-free for a period of time after the deceased's death.

Overall, barring serious calamity, Sam and Sue's assets will probably have grown to a significant size as they have aged. That means instead of worrying about having enough to support the family if one of them dies, they may want to look at ways to reduce their estates to make sure that their sons will not have to pay estate taxes upon their deaths.

Since assets in revocable trusts are sheltered from federal estate taxes, Sam and Sue might want to put their savings into revocable trusts – trusts they can change during their lifetimes – listing each other as beneficiaries. They may also choose to lower the size of their estate by increasing their charitable donations, creating scholarships in their names or looking at other ways of giving back to their community, as well as other forms of giving.

Since each of them can give a tax-free gift up to $13,000 a year in cash, stocks, real estate, or shares in a company to whomever he or she wishes or can pay anyone's tuition or medical expenses, as long as payment is made directly to the provider, Sam and Sue could pay a grandchild's college tuition and also give that grandchild $26,000 each year ($13,000 from each of them.)

If they were concerned about making an outright gift to a grandchild (because they want the money used for a limited purpose, such as college) then they could set up a trust for each grandchild and put their money there each year instead.

CONCLUSION

If you are like most readers of how-to and self-help books, there is a good chance that after you put this book down you still will not begin your estate planning. You have taken the time to read this book. Now it is time to begin to put a plan in place that will protect yourself and your family. Follow the steps outlined in the chapters and make it a goal to secure your future.

Glossary

accountant A professional who audits records and prepares tax returns and financial reports.

adl's (activities of daily living) Normal, everyday functions, such as bathing, eating, getting dressed, or going to the bathroom that one can usually do without assistance.

administrator, administratrix The person appointed by the court to manage your estate if you die without a will.

adult day care Supervised social activities or custodial care for the elderly, usually at a senior or community center.

alimony Periodic payments made by a divorced spouse to his/her ex-spouse for support, by agreement or court order. Typically, alimony can be modified or amended and terminates when the person receiving it cohabits with another, remarries, or dies.

alimony trust A trust established as part of the divorce agreement, into which cash, investment assets or business assets are transferred before the alimony payments are due. The trust then pays out the required amount of money for the alimony payments.

annual exclusion amount The maximum amount of money (up to $13,000 presently) a person can give each year to anyone the donor wishes without having to pay a gift tax. This amount will be gradually adjusted upward for inflation.

annuities Contracts between a financial institution and you which allow you to invest money that grows on a tax deferred basis. You may make payments at once or over time. The company promises to make payments to you – either for a specific time period or over your lifetime. No state or federal taxes are due as the money accumulates. When the funds are distributed to you they are taxed.

applicable exclusion amount The amount of money in your estate (currently set at $5,000,000) you are permitted to leave to your heirs free of federal estate tax. This was formerly known as the applicable unified credit amount.

applicable unified credit (See *applicable exclusion amount*.)

agent The person named in a durable power of attorney or health care proxy to act on behalf of the principal, or person establishing the durable power of attorney or health care proxy.

assets Any property (tangible, intangible or real) you own which composes your wealth.

assisted living facility A residential arrangement that combines normal apartment-style living with personal and health care services for people who need some assistance.

"at-home" rider An addition to a long term care insurance policy that changes the provisions of the contract in order to provide coverage for the insured while living at home.

attorney-in-fact (See Agent.)

basis, income tax The amount you paid for an asset. If the asset is real estate, your basis is reduced by depreciation and increased by improvements. If you received the asset by gift, you take over the donor's income tax basis. (For assets received at death see *stepped-up income tax basis*.)

beneficiary (primary, secondary) A person, trust or organization you designate to receive property at your death. You must name a primary (first taker) beneficiary for any life insurance policy, annuity, retirement plan, and bank or investment account you hold. The secondary beneficiary you designate is the person, trust or organization you designate to take the assets if the primary beneficiary is not then living.

beneficiary (trust. The persons or organizations designated in the trust document to receive or benefit from assets.

bequest An asset, such as money or personal property, left to a person, institution, or other entity in your will or trust.

brokerage account An investment account opened at a brokerage firm.

bypass trust A trust established in the estate plan of the first spouse to die that gives the surviving spouse the amount sheltered from tax by the applicable unified credit, but places it into a trust the spouse controls while he/she survives, but which will not be treated as something the spouse owns when he/she dies, thereby avoiding ("bypassing") future estate taxes.

buy-sell agreement An agreement between partners or among stockholders of a business in which they agree that in the event of the death, disability or retirement of one of them, the others will buy out his/her interest at a certain price (which can be annually adjusted) and according to certain terms.

capital gains tax The income tax you pay (when an asset is sold) on the amount the asset has increased in value since you bought it. The gain is the difference between the original cost of the asset and its ultimate sale price.

charitable bequest A gift of money or other property to a charity under a will or trust.

charitable gift annuity A lifetime income gift in which you transfer your assets to the charity now, receive a charitable deduction for a portion of the transfer and you or a beneficiary receives income for the rest of your life or for a fixed period of time.

charitable lead trust A trust whose income flows first to a designated charitable organization, for a stated number of years, and then to family members.

charitable remainder trust A trust whose income flows first to family members or another designated person. Upon the death of the beneficiary, the remaining assets in the trust pass to the charitable organization.

Clayton Q-Tip trust A Q-Tip trust in which after one spouse's death an independent trustee decides how much money passes to the trust for the surviving spouse and how much passes to the children (or to a trust for their benefit).

codicil A separate legal document which, after it is signed and properly witnessed, changes an existing will.

comdex A composite of all the ratings that a life insurance company has received. The comdex ranks a company, on a scale of 1 to 100, in relation to its ratings and those of other companies rated by at least two of the top rating services (A.M. Best, Standard & Poors, Moody's Investor Service, Fitch).

common law marriage In a minority of states couples are considered married if they live together and think of themselves as husband and wife.

community foundation A tax-exempt public charity that helps a region through the contributions of individuals, families, businesses, and organizations who share the common concern of improving the quality of life in their area,. A community foundation is overseen by a volunteer board and distributes money to local charitable organizations.

community property Property acquired during marriage, other than by gift or inheritance, that is legally presumed, in certain states, to be the product of the joint effort of both spouses.

community property affidavit A written notarized statement that confirms all property held in your name and your spouse's name is community property.

continuing care retirement community A residential arrangement in which residents can receive gradually increasing attention and care as their needs increase with age or infirmity.

convertibility option An opportunity in a life insurance contract to convert term insurance to more permanent life insurance, in many cases without a medical examination.

co-tenancy When two or more persons own the same property at the same time.

co-tenant One of the property owners in a co-tenancy.

co-trustee A person or institution who serves with the trustee to help make decisions on the administration of the trust.

cross purchase agreement (See *buy-sell agreement.*) An agreement under which each partner or shareholder agrees with each of the other partners or shareholders to buy out his or her interest in the business in the event of death. This type of agreement is usually backed up by life insurance.

custodian A person or institution named to care for property held under the Uniform Gifts To Minors Act or the Uniform Transfers to Minors Act.

deed The legal document by which a person transfers legal title of real estate to another person.

disability insurance Insurance purchased to provide income if you are no longer able to work due to injury or illness.

disclaimer The right to refuse to accept property left to you by gift, joint ownership, your designation as a beneficiary, a will, or a trust.

disclaimed assets The assets you refuse to accept by disclaimer.

disclaimer will A will in which the assets are left to the surviving spouse and the surviving spouse has nine months after death to decide how much to keep and how much to "disclaim" for tax reasons and pass to a trust for the children.

discretionary trust A trust that gives the trustee the authority to decide how much to distribute to beneficiaries on an ongoing basis.

donee The recipient of a gift.

donor The person who makes the gift.

donor-advised fund A fund offered by some major financial institutions and some charities that allows the donor or others designated by the donor to make recommendations regarding proposed charitable distributions. Contributions to a donor advised fund are deductible from income tax (subject to certain limitations), and are not liable for capital gains tax when the fund sells the asset.

durable power of attorney A document in which you give another person the authority to handle your financial affairs. The powers remain effective through any disability or incapacity you may have.

dynasty trust An irrevocable trust designed to last for several generations (and in some states forever). (See *generation skipping trust* and *rule against perpetuities*.)

estate Your *taxable* estate includes the total value, usually the fair market value, of all possessions - property and debts - you own at your death. Your *probate* estate includes any asset that is in your name alone at your death. It does not include assets you own jointly with a right of survivorship, assets that are already titled in the name of your trust, assets such as a life insurance policy, or annuity or retirement planning asset that pass to beneficiaries by contract. You can have a significant taxable estate and totally avoid probate

estate planning What this book is about – protecting yourself when you are alive, if you are disabled and protecting your beneficiaries at your death in a tax-efficient manner.

estate taxes. Taxes imposed by the federal and some state governments at your death on the assets you have left to others.

equitable distribution states Those states in which divorce law divides property acquired by the spouses during marriage based on such factors as relative financial investments, contributions as a homemaker and respective needs. Title to property in either spouse's name does not necessarily restrict the court's right to award that property to the other spouse as part of equitable division.

E.R.I.S.A (Employee Retirement Security Act) A 1974 law governing the operation of most private pension and benefit plans.

escrow The delivery of documents or assets to a third person to be held by him or her until a certain condition agreed upon in advance is met. Upon the occurrence of that event the escrow property is delivered to the party as provided in the original agreement.

executor, executrix The person or corporation appointed by the court to handle the administration of your estate.

fair market value The price at which an item would be sold at retail by a willing buyer to a willing seller if neither party were under any compulsion to buy or sell.

fiduciary Anyone responsible for the management of another's property, including executor, administrator, trustee, guardian or conservator.

financial planner A person you hire to evaluate your personal finances and define with you your tax and financial goals. A financial planner may have professional designations and certifications. Sometimes a financial planner charges by fee; other times by a age of your assets.

fraudulent conveyance The transfer of your assets with an intent to deceive a creditor.

funding of trust The process by which you transfer and retitle the assets into the name of the trust to avoid probate.

gap coverage (Also known as *Medigap insurance* or *Medicare supplement insurance*.) Medical insurance designed to supplement Medicare's benefits by covering some of the costs for services not covered by Medicare.

generation-skipping tax A tax applied when assets are transferred to a recipient (outright or in trust) more than a single generation removed from the transferor. For example, when a grandmother transfers assets to a grandchild.

generation-skipping trust A trust funded with the generation-skipping exemption amount that will pass on to your grandchildren's generation without being subject to estate tax at your children's death.

geriatric care manager An independent professional hired to help establish a plan of care, and select both caregivers and service providers for an elderly patient.

gifting The process of donating your assets to another person or organization during your lifetime.

gift tax A tax imposed by the federal government, and, in a few states, the state government, on assets given away during your lifetime.

gift tax exclusion The maximum amount of assets (currently $1,000,000) you can give to individuals during your lifetime free of gift taxes.

gross estate The value of your entire taxable estate without taking into account any deductions or credits.

guardian of the property The court appointed person or corporation responsible for handling the financial affairs of a minor or an incompetent person.

guardian of the person The court appointed person or corporation responsible for handling the personal care of a minor or an incompetent person.

health care power of attorney A legal document that specifies the type of medical treatment and life support you want if you are disabled or incapacitated and unable to make the decision yourself. It allows a person of your choosing to make the decision on your behalf.

health care proxy (See *health care power of attorney*.) A Health Care Proxy may or may not contain language pertaining to life support.

heir at law The persons who are entitled by state law to inherit your estate if you do not leave a will.

HEMS (health, education, maintenance, support) The typical standard in an irrevocable trust by which the Trustee decides whether or not a beneficiary should receive funds. This standard allows the Trustee who is also a beneficiary to exercise discretion and keep the trust property out of the trustee-beneficiary's taxable estate.

HIPPA The Health Insurance Portability and Accountability Act of 1996 (known as "HIPPA". Under HIPPA, if you do not expressly waive your right to privacy in writing hospitals and physicians do not have the legal right to speak with your health care agent or to release medical information to that person.

home equity conversion mortgage (See *reverse mortgage*.)

homestead exemption The value of your primary residence allowed by state law which is protected from your creditors. In most states this protection is afforded only if you have filed a homestead declaration.

insurance professional An agent who is licensed by the state to sell life insurance, disability insurance, long term care insurance, and other financial products.

insured A person covered by life, disability, long term care, or other insurance policies.

Internal Revenue Code of 1986 Legislation passed by Congress that specifies which income and assets are to be taxed and which may be deducted from the tax.

Internal Revenue Service The federal governmental agency that is responsible for the administration and collection of federal taxes. It is part of the U.S. Treasury. The IRS prints and distributes tax forms and examines and audits returns.

intestate succession The way in which your estate will pass under state law if you die without a will.

IRA (Individual Retirement Account) An account you establish that offers tax benefits for saving for retirement. Contributions to it are tax deductible and the money in it accumulates interest tax free until withdrawn at retirement, at which point the money is subject to income tax.

irrevocable trust A trust that cannot be changed, amended or revoked.

irrevocable life insurance trust An irrevocable trust that owns and is the primary designated beneficiary of life insurance, so that the life insurance proceeds are removed from the insured's taxable estate.

issue Your direct descendants – children, grandchildren and more remote descendants.

joint ownership Sharing the ownership of property and agreeing that at the death of one joint owner the property passes on to the other.

Keough plan A retirement plan established by a self-employed person or a partnership.

key man life insurance A life insurance policy on a key employee that is owned by and payable to the business. The intent is to provide the business with operating funds to hire a replacement for the key employee if he dies while employed.

level term life insurance (See *term insurance*.) The premiums stay fixed or "level" for a specified number of years, typically 5, 10, 20 or 30 years.

life estate The right to use property and receive income from it during one's lifetime.

life insurance A contract between an individual and an insurance company obligating the company to pay a specific and agreed upon sum of money on the death of the insured.

lifetime transfers Assets you give away during your lifetime.

limited liability company (LLC) A business entity formed under state law that is taxed as a sole proprietorship or partnership and has creditor protection similar to that of a corporation.

liquid assets Assets that can be easily sold and converted to cash.

liquidate (a business) To sell or dissolve the business.

living trust A trust you establish during your lifetime. (See *Trusts*.)

living will A document in which you specify that you do not want to have your life artificially prolonged by technical means.

long term care insurance Insurance that covers the cost of continual custodial care in either a nursing home, other institutional setting or the policy holder's home.

marital deduction A tax deduction that allows spouses who are United States citizens to transfer unlimited amounts of assets to one another (in most states), both when they are alive and at the death of one.

marital deduction trust A trust established to receive an amount of assets for the surviving spouse's benefit that qualifies for the marital deduction. (See also *Q-TIP Trust*.)

Meals on Wheels Association of America A nonprofit association that provides food services to those in need, shut-ins and the elderly.

Medicaid A joint federal/state government program which pays for medical care for the disabled and the financially needy.

Medicare A federal program administered by the Social Security Administration which provides medical benefits to those over the age of 65 regardless of financial need.

Monte Carlo simulation A complex mathematical technique that tests your financial plan by running hundreds or hundreds of thousands of simulations (taking into account such varying factors as your possible rates of return on investments and both interest and inflation rates) to estimate the probability of your being able to meet your financial goals in the future.

non-durable power of attorney A power of attorney that is revoked when you become disabled or incapacitated or die.

personal property Any property other than real estate.

pooled income fund A trust established by a public charity that enables a donor (or a person the donor designates) to receive income from the trust for the rest of his/her life, with the understanding that when the donor (or donor-designatee) dies, the value of the trust goes to charity.

portability Under the new federal gift and estate tax law, the $5,000,000 exemption is portable between spouses (although there are restrictions on the dollar amount if the person has been married more than one time). That means that even if the first spouse to die does not establish or fund a trust, his or her $5,000,000 exemption can be applied and used when the surviving spouse dies. It is not clear whether or not this portability provision will extend past the year 2012. The portability exemption of the first spouse is not adjusted for inflation so even if the portability provisions are extended past 2012, under the current law if there is any passage of time between the date of the death of the first spouse and the surviving spouse the $5,000,000 is locked in. In addition, as of now, no state allows portability of the state death tax exemption so although portability may benefit those with a federal estate tax it will not benefit those with a state estate tax.

pour-over will A will used in conjunction with a trust that specifies that any assets either intentionally or inadvertently left out of the trust should be "poured into" or added to the trust at the time of death to prevent the creation of an intestate estate.

postnuptial agreement An agreement signed by you and your spouse after you are married which sets forth how your income and assets will be divided when the marriage terminates, either by divorce or by death.

prenuptial agreement An agreement signed by you and your fiancé before the marriage which sets forth how your income and assets will be divided when the marriage terminates, either by divorce or by death.

private charitable foundation A family or corporate foundation engaged in charitable activities. Stricter contribution rules apply here than apply to public charities, as do penalties and excise taxes.

probate The legal, court-supervised process of administering your estate at death or legal disability if you have not made provisions yourself by engaging in the estate planning process.

probate court The court which supervises the probate process. (Sometimes known as *Surrogate's Court*.)

probate property Assets which are administered at your death through the probate process. Usually these are assets which are in your name alone at your death.

proprietary reverse mortgage A reverse mortgage that is offered by a bank mortgage company or other private lender and backed by the companies that develop them.

public sector loans Loans provided by governmental agencies.

Qualified Terminable Interest Property (QTIP). A trust (especially useful in second marriages where the grantor desires to provide for a second spouse, but wants the trust assets to be distributed to his/her children upon the spouse's death) established for the benefit of a spouse that qualifies for the unlimited marital deduction and controls where the trust assets pass at the surviving spouse's death.

real property Real estate.

residue The property given by your will or revocable trust to your beneficiaries after all specific gifts have been made and all administration expenses and taxes have been paid.

retirement planning asset Tax-deferred assets such as qualified pension and profit sharing plans, IRA's, Keoughs plans and some annuities.

retitling assets (See *Funding of Trusts*.)

reverse mortgage A loan that enables an owner to borrow against the equity in his/her residence in either a lump sum or periodic payments and defers the repayment of the loan until either the residence is sold or the owner dies.

revocable trust (See *living trust*.)

right of survivorship The right of a co-owner of a property (not a tenant in common) to take the entire asset if he survives the other joint owner.

rule against perpetuities A rule of law that limits how long an irrevocable trust can be in effect (other than charitable trusts which can last forever). In many states irrevocable trusts cannot continue for more than about 90 years; in other states they can continue forever.

separate property Property belonging to one spouse in which the other spouse generally has no claim.

settlor The person who establishes the trust. Sometimes known as donor or grantor.

Sinatra clause A statement in a will or trust providing that any beneficiary who challenges the document or how it is administered will forfeit his inheritance. This is binding in most states and is also known as an in terrorem clause.

"special needs" (children) Children with disabilities who need assistance with physical, cognitive, emotional or learning skills.

special needs trust A trust established for disabled persons who may or will require governmental assistance. The trust provisions benefit the person, yet do not jeopardize eligibility for governmental benefits.

spendthrift trust A trust that includes provisions which protect a trust beneficiary's interest from the claims of creditors.

spray provision A trust provision which allows the trustee to make discretionary distributions of income or principal among a class of beneficiaries. (Also known as a *sprinkling provision*.)

springing durable power of attorney A durable power of attorney that becomes effective only upon your disability or incapacity.

stepped-up income tax basis An increased tax cost in property that takes place at a person's death when the asset is included in his federal taxable estate and is appraised at the current fair market value (rather than at the amount the person originally paid for the asset).

subtrusts Trusts established in a master trust document which become operational at a subsequent time. For example, the first spouse to die's trust may break into two trusts: a marital trust and a bypass trust at death.

successor guardian The person or organization who takes over as guardian if the original guardian resigns, dies or is incapacitated.

sunset clause A clause in a contract which specifies when the contract will expire or terminate.

taking against the will The ability of a surviving spouse to choose a statutorily allocated share of the decedent's assets rather than taking what the will or revocable trust provides for the surviving spouse's benefit. In some states the surviving spouse is entitled to take an allocated share of the augmented estate which includes joint assets and life insurance.

tangible personal property Property other than real estate and other than investments that can be touched – such as cars, furniture, jewelry, clothing, books, antiques, etc.

tax A rate or sum of money assessed against a person, property or activity for the support of the government.

taxable estate Your gross estate less deductions and administration expenses.

tenancy by the entirety A form of joint ownership between a husband and wife with a right of survivorship, so that when one spouse dies the other spouse automatically owns the asset. In most states if the parties divorce the ownership is converted to a tenancy in common.

tenancy in common A type of ownership where two or more people share a property, but not necessarily equally, and although each one has the right to use the entire property, there is no right of survivorship. Any party may petition the court for a sale of property and have the proceeds divided. At the death of one owner, the other owners do not automatically inherit.

term life insurance Life insurance intended to be in place for a short period of time, subject to renewal at the end of the term at a premium increase based on the increased age of the insured at the time.

testamentary By or under a will.

testate Dying with a will.

testator The person who makes a will.

transfer tax structure (See *tax*.) A tax levied when the asset is given away, either when the donor is living (gift tax), at death (estate tax) or when it skips a generation (generation skipping tax).

trust A legal entity you (as grantor, donor or settler) establish to manage assets. Some ("revocable trusts") can be changed. Others ("irrevocable trusts") cannot be changed. If the trust is established during your lifetime it is known as an inter vivos or living trust. If the trust is established in your will it is known as a testamentary trust.

trust property The assets held in your trust. Also known as trust res or trust principal.

trustee The person or institution who manages trust property according to the terms of the trust.

unified credit A tax credit which may be applied toward gift or estate tax. (See *applicable exclusion amount*.)

Uniform Transfers (or Gifts) to Minors Act (UGMA/UTMA) A law adopted by most states that sets up rules for the distribution and administration of assets in the name of a child.

universal life insurance A flexible premium life insurance policy under which the policy holder may change the death benefit, vary the amount or timing of premium payments and choose the investment vehicles for premiums. The premiums (less expense charges and commissions) are credited to a policy account from which mortality charges are deducted and to which interest is credited at a rate that may change.

unlimited marital deduction. (See *marital deduction.*)

variable universal life insurance   A life insurance policy which blends the features found in both variable life and universal life policies. It offers a choice of underlying investment accounts, flexible premiums and an adjustable death benefit – which may rise or fall depending on the success of the underlying investments you choose.

Visiting Nurse Association   A not-for-profit community-based home care and hospice provider. Its mission is to provide professional and compassionate health care in your home and community. It brings care to people of all ages confronted by disease, disability or death.

will   A formal legal document which specifies who will administer your estate and how it will be distributed at your death.

whole life insurance   Life insurance that is in effect as long as premiums are paid up until the death of the policy holder. (Also known as *"permanent life insurance."*)

Wealth Assessment Exhibit
Information Gathering

Estate planning is a broad, multifaceted process guided by a series of basic strategies. But if it is to be effective, your estate plan must also be highly individualized, specifically designed to deal with your unique financial and familial needs, wants and goals. And before you can communicate your needs, wants and goals to an estate planner, you have to figure them out for yourself.

This questionnaire is designed to help you do just that by amassing the data needed to tailor a plan that is a "perfect fit" for you and those you care about. This questionnaire is set forth twice – the first questionnaire is geared toward married couples, partners and unmarried couples. The second version of the questionnaire is geared toward single, divorced and widowed women. You should complete the appropriate version of the questionnaire.

DATE QUESTIONNAIRE FOR MARRIED COUPLES, PARTNERS AND UNMARRIED COUPLES

I. Family Information (please use full names)

Husband/Partner		Wife/Partner				
Date of Birth		Date of Birth				
S.S. No.		S.S. No.				
Work Phone		Work Phone				
Home Address						
Home Phone		Fax		U.S. Citizen?	H	W

(Note: It is very important to complete the "children" section as thoroughly as possible, including children born to you, adopted by you while you were married to your current spouse, children born to or adopted by you when you were married to a pervious spouse, and children born to or adopted by you when you were not married. In virtually all states, adopted and natural born children have inheritance rights unless they are specifically excluded in the will by name. You should not name stepchildren that you have not adopted, since they are not entitled by law to a share of your property when you die, as they are not your legal heirs. If you choose to leave assets to stepchildren or their issue, they must be specifically included in the documents.)

	CHILDREN					
Name						
S.S. No.						
Date of Birth						
Address						
Marital Status						
Grandchildren	Name	DOB	Name	DOB	Name	DOB
First						
Second						
Third						

a) Are any of your children or grandchildren adopted? If so, who.

(Note: Under current law in just about every state, adopted offspring are treated as blood relatives in estate planning unless they are specifically excluded. With the rise of non-traditional families, this is going to become an increasingly important question.)

b) Do you have any other dependents? If so, please explain. (Note: This answer will help determine how much income your estate has to generate in order to take care of those you are supporting now and those who will depend on you later – your parents, siblings, disabled sibling, spouse's family members, etc.)

_____

_____

_____

c) Date and place of your marriage

_____

d) Do you have a prenuptial or postnuptial agreement?

_____

e) Any changes of state of residence during marriage? If so, please name each state and indicate year of arrival.

(Note: Geography is important in estate planning. If you live in a community property state, for example, the rights you have to the assets and income of your partner may be quite different than if you live in a common law state. State laws also vary on asset protection from creditors, and who can or can't act as trustee.)

_____

f) Are husband and wife both U.S. citizens? _____

If no, please indicate citizenship and visa status in U.S. _____

(Note: If both or one is not a United States citizen, then the unlimited marital deduction rules which allow all of the assets to pass to the surviving spouse and not incur any federal gift or estate taxes do not apply. The theory behind this is that if a U.S. citizen leaves all assets to a U.S. citizen spouse and then dies, the taxes would be deferred but the government would get its taxes when the surviving U.S. citizen spouse died. A non-U.S. citizen spouse, on the other hand, might leave the country and take all assets out of the taxing authorities jurisdiction, and therefore it is too risky for the federal government to allow the same tax deferral.)

g) Previous marriages for either spouse? ( ) Yes ( ) No   If yes, please list:

(Note: This question is designed to uncover any assets or obligations. If a prior spouse died, was there a trust set up in his or her estate plan to benefit the surviving spouse which should be reviewed? If a marriage terminated in divorce, does the divorcee have ongoing obligations under the divorce accord, such as maintaining life insurance for alimony and/or child support? Is the ownership or beneficiary of life insurance or retirement plans already committed, so that transferring that ownership would violate court orders?)

H/W   Previous spouse's name _____
How and when did marriage terminate? (e.g., death, divorce)

_____

_____

_____

h) Additional family circumstances:

(Note: This is the place to mention any disabled or special needs children or health issues you have that might affect your ability to get life insurance or long term care.)

_____

_____

_____

II. Income/Employment

	HUSBAND	WIFE
Occupation	$ /year	$ /year
Salary	$ /year	$ /year
Net Rental Income	$ /year	$ /year
Dividends/ Interest	$ /year	$ /year
Pension	$ /year	$ /year
Social Security	$ /year	$ /year
Other Income (1)	$ /year	$ /year
Other Income (2)	$ /year	$ /year
Approximate Total Annual Income	$ /year	$ /year

III. Assets

a. Real Estate (List additional properties on a separate schedule.)

LOCATION (Indicate "R" if rental)	APPROXIMATE VALUE	MORTGAGE BALANCE	FORM OF OWNERSHIP (Joint, Individual, Trust, etc.)
1.	$	$	
2.	$	$	
3.	$	$	
4.	$	$	
5.	$	$	
6.	$	$	
7.	$	$	
8.	$	$	
totals:	$	$	

b. Bank Accounts, CDs, Money Market Accounts: (List additional properties on a separate schedule.)

TYPE OF ASSET SAVINGS, CHECKING, CD ETC.	APPROXIMATE BALANCE	NAME(S) ON ACCOUNTS
1.	$	
2.	$	
3.	$	
4.	$	
5.	$	
approximate total:	$	

c. Stocks, Bonds & Other Investments: (It is not necessary to list the individual stocks, bonds, etc.)

TYPE OF ASSETS (Stocks, Bonds, Mutual Funds, Treasury Bills, Single Premium Annuities, etc.)	APPROXIMATE VALUE	NAME(S) ON SECURITIES OR BROKERAGE ACCOUNTS
1.	$	
2.	$	
3.	$	
4.	$	
5.	$	
6.	$	
approximate total:	$	

d. Life Insurance:

Person Insured				
Face Value	$	$	$	$
Cash Value/Loan	$	$	$	$
Beneficiary				
Owner of the Policy				
Type of Policy (Term or Permanent) and Name of Company				

Total Life Insurance (Face Value):

Husband	$	Wife	$

e. Pension, Profit Sharing, IRA, Keough, or Other Retirement Plans:

TYPE OF PLAN (IRA, KEOGH, PENSION, TIAA, ETC.)	CURRENT VALUE	PARTICIPANT/BENEFICIARY
1.	$	/
2.	$	/
3.	$	/
4.	$	/

Total Lump Sum Retirement Plan Value

Husband	$	Wife	$

f. Business Interests (owned by husband or wife):

If either of you owns any interest in a closely held business, attach a statement indicating: (1) Type of business; (2) Form of business; (e.g., corporation, partnership, or sole proprietorship); (3) Your share of the business; (4) Your position in the business; (5) Other owners, their shares and relationship to you; (6) Whether there is a buy/sell agreement; and (7) Desired disposition of your share.

(Note: This is an opportunity to discuss the business, its succession and its value in the context of estate planning so that a spouse who is not the business owner can get a realistic handle on what the value of the business is and what can be expected in the event of the owner's death.)

Your Estimate of Value of the Business

Husband	$	Wife	$

g. Miscellaneous:

(i.e., expected inheritances, valuable personal property, promissory notes payable to you, any other special factors which may affect your situation).

(Note: This is designed to highlight when the plan may have to be changed or revised. If, for example, if you are expecting an additional inheritance when your parents or grandparents die, then the plan may have to be completely revamped at that time.)

_____

_____

_____

_____

h. Prior Gifts:

(Itemize significant past gifts [over $13,000/yr.] to any one individual made by either of you. Indicate whether you filed gift tax returns.)

(Note: This is important to keep track of, because once you go past the $13,000 per year annual exclusion then - with the exceptions of making a gift for anyone's medical or educational expenses and making such payments directly to the provider - you are making a taxable gift. Also, once you go through your federal lifetime gifting allotment (currently $5,000,000), you reduce the amount that could pass tax free at your death.)

_____

_____

_____

_____

i. Assets of Minor Children

If you have any minor children, state whether any such child has separate assets (such as custodial accounts), including approximate amounts and in whose name they are held.

(Note: This information will enable your estate planner to determine whether the sums are enough for future tuition, on one hand, and, on the other hand, and if the accounts in the children's names might be "overfunded" – whether the children will have too much money to do with as they please when they reach the age of 21.)

_____

_____

_____

_____

IV. Liabilities

Indicate significant debts and debts guaranteed by you (excluding mortgages listed earlier), as well as lawsuits, or claims, present or anticipated.

(Note: If there are significant mortgages or personal guarantees, it is important to know which member of the couple is obligated on them, and whether a life insurance policy needs to be put in place to cover those liabilities if personal assets are at risk. Sometimes the commercial financing institutions will mandate that these liabilities be covered by life insurance.)

Total Liabilities

Husband	$	Wife	$	Joint	$

V. Financial Recap

Please list the total values from Items III A to G:

(Note: Putting a financial recap together and discussing it is very important and should be done on a regular basis. Knowing how assets are titled – whose name is on what – raises key estate planning issues. In many states, for example, if an asset is titled by joint owner-ship with a right of survivorship or as tenants by the entirety, it will pass to the surviving joint owner regardless of what your will says. It is important also to highlight assets here that are owned jointly with others – people who are not married to each other – and property that is owned as tenants in common without a survivorship right.)

	HUSBAND	WIFE	JOINT/TRUST
Real Estate	$	$	$
Bank Assets	$	$	$
Stocks, etc.	$	$	$
Retirement	$	$	$
Insurance	$	$	$
Business	$	$	$
Miscellaneous	$	$	$
Totals	$	$	$
Liabilities (Including Mortgages)	$ ( )	$ ( )	$ ( )
Net Assets	$	$	$

VI: Planning Issues

a. Your Goals:

Please briefly state your estate planning goals (e.g. tax minimization, financial well-being of spouse/partner, education of children):

_____

_____

b. Long Term Care Insurance

Long term care insurance can help prevent the depletion of your assets if you should ever require nursing home or other long term care, including care in your home.

Are you currently covered by a long term care insurance policy? _____

If so, please submit a copy of your policy and any explanatory or descriptive literature you may have received.

If you are not covered, would you like to discuss long term care insurance?

c. Disability Insurance

Are you covered by a disability insurance policy? _____

If yes: Amount of coverage _____

Waiting period _____

Duration of benefit _____

If you are not covered, would you like to discuss disability insurance coverage? _____

VII. Disposition of Assets: Explain in a general way how you wish to dispose of your property (desired shares for children, relatives, charity, etc.)

(Note: Thinking through these issues ahead of time – how much you wish your children, nieces, nephews, other relatives to receive, who is to be primary beneficiary, who needs special protection – will highlight any areas of disagreement and make a discussion to iron out the differences more productive.)

_____

_____

_____

_____

_____

VIII. Fiduciaries

Whom are you considering as possible candidates to serve as your Executor or Trustee, and Guardian of your minor children?

(Note: In many instances either husband or wife or both can be the initial trustee (s) of the respective trusts; But even if this is your choice, you should still think about the selection of a successor. Giving some thought to the fiduciary decision in advance of the initial meeting – even if you are not really sure – provides a jump start to the discussion. In the guardian arena, for example, it forces you to put down a name. For many couples this is a stumbling block, either because there is no clear choice or because they do not agree. Having broached the subject on their own and then brought it to the meeting will make the meeting more productive as the estate planner is then in better position to facilitate a discussion as to who should be selected.)

Executor(s)		Address	
Successor Executor(s)		Address	
Guardian(s)		Address	
Successor Guardian(s)		Address	
Trustee(s)		Address	
Successor Trustee(s)		Address	

IX. Your Professional Advisors

(Note: For couples, it is important that each one has all this information at hand. It is also good to have each advisor know who the other advisors are. In many circumstances, such as when there is a family business involved, it helps to have the advisors meet as a team — annually or more frequently. Having the entire team together in dialogue can lead to open discussions and a better result.)

Accountant		Telephone	
Attorney		Telephone	
Insurance Advisor		Telephone	
Financial Planner		Telephone	
Stockbroker		Telephone	

X. Safe Deposit

Safe deposit box location and persons having access:

_____

XI. Additional Comments/Questions Include below any additional comments, concerns, information, or specific questions you wish to have answered in the estate planning process:

_____

_____

_____

_____

XII. Please attach photocopies of the following documents: Attached (X) or N/A

Wills and codicils, if any: _____

Trust Instruments in which you have an interest: _____

Deeds to Real Estate: _____

Most, recent Federal and State Income Tax Returns: _____

All Gift Tax Returns: _____

Pre or Post Nuptial Agreements: _____

Separation Agreements, Divorce Papers: _____

Life Insurance Policies: _____

Business Agreements and Documents
regarding Interests in Closely Held Business: _____

Retirement Plans or Other Information from
Plan Administrator: _____

DATA QUESTIONNAIRE FOR SINGLE, DIVORCED AND WIDOWED WOMEN

I. Family Information (please use full names)

Husband/Partner					
Date of Birth					
S.S. No.					
Work Phone					
Home Address					
Home Phone		Fax		U.S. Citizen?	

(Note: It is very important to complete the "children" section as thoroughly as possible, including children born to you, adopted by you while you were married to your current spouse, children born to or adopted by you when you were married to a pervious spouse, and children born to or adopted by you when you were not married. In virtually all states, adopted and natural born children have inheritance rights unless they are specifically ex-cluded in the will by name. You should not name stepchildren that you have not adopted, since they are not entitled by law to a share of your property when you die, as they are not your legal heirs. If you choose to leave assets to stepchildren or their issue, they must be specifically included in the documents.)

CHILDREN						
Name						
S.S. No.						
Date of Birth						
Address						
Marital Status						
Grandchildren	Name	DOB	Name	DOB	Name	DOB
First						
Second						
Third						

a) Are any of your children or grandchildren adopted? If so, who.

(Note: Under current law in just about every state, adopted offspring are treated as blood relatives in estate planning unless they are specifically excluded. With the rise of non-traditional families, this is going to become an increasingly important question.)

---

b) Do you have any other dependents? If so, please explain. (Note: This answer will help determine how much income your estate has to generate in order to take care of those you are supporting now and those who will depend on you later – your parents, siblings, disabled sibling, spouse's family members, etc.)

---

c) Are you a U.S. citizen? If no, please indicate citizenship and visa status in U.S

_____

(Note: If you are not a United States citizen then certain treaties may apply to the taxation of your assets)

d) Previous marriages? ( ) Yes ( ) No   If yes, please list

(Note: This question is designed to uncover any assets or obligations. If a prior spouse died, was there a trust set up in his or her estate plan to benefit the surviving spouse which should be reviewed? If a marriage terminated in divorce, does the divorcee have ongoing obligations under the divorce accord, such as maintaining life insurance for alimony and/or child support? Is the ownership or beneficiary of life insurance or retirement plans already committed, so that transferring that ownership would violate court orders?)

Previous spouse's name   **How and when did marriage terminate? (e.g., death, divorce)**

_____

_____

_____

h) Additional family circumstances:

(Note: This is the place to mention any disabled or special needs children or health issues you have that might affect your ability to get life insurance or long term care.)

_____

_____

_____

_____

II. Income/Employment

Occupation	$ /year
Salary	$ /year
Net Rental Income	$ /year
Dividends/ Interest	$ /year
Pension	$ /year
Social Security	$ /year
Other Income (1)	$ /year
Other Income (2)	$ /year
Approximate Total Annual Income	$ /year

III. Assets

a. Real Estate (List additional properties on a separate schedule.)

LOCATION (Indicate "R" if rental)	APPROXIMATE VALUE	MORTGAGE BALANCE	FORM OF OWNERSHIP (Joint, Individual, Trust, etc.)
1.	$	$	
2.	$	$	
3.	$	$	
4.	$	$	
5.	$	$	
6.	$	$	
7.	$	$	
8.	$	$	
totals:	$	$	

b. Bank Accounts, CDs, Money Market Accounts: (List additional properties on a separate schedule.)

TYPE OF ASSET SAVINGS, CHECKING, CD ETC.	APPROXIMATE BALANCE	NAME(S) ON ACCOUNTS
1.	$	
2.	$	
3.	$	
4.	$	
5.	$	
approximate total:	$	

c. Stocks, Bonds & Other Investments: (It is not necessary to list the individual stocks, bonds, etc.)

TYPE OF ASSETS (Stocks, Bonds, Mutual Funds, Treasury Bills, Single Premium Annuities, etc.)	APPROXIMATE VALUE	NAME(S) ON SECURITIES OR BROKERAGE ACCOUNTS
1.	$	
2.	$	
3.	$	
4.	$	
5.	$	
6.	$	
approximate total:	$	

d. Life Insurance:

Person Insured				
Face Value	$	$	$	$
Cash Value/Loan	$	$	$	$
Beneficiary				
Owner of the Policy				
Type of Policy (Term or Permanent) and Name of Company				

Total Life Insurance (Face Value):

Husband	$

e. Pension, Profit Sharing, IRA, Keough, or Other Retirement Plans:

TYPE OF PLAN (IRA, KEOGH, PENSION, TIAA, ETC.)	CURRENT VALUE	PARTICIPANT/BENEFICIARY
1.	$	/
2.	$	/
3.	$	/
4.	$	/

Total Lump Sum Retirement Plan Value

$

f. Business Interests (owned by husband or wife):

If either of you owns any interest in a closely-held business, attach a statement indicating: (1) Type of Business; (2) Form of business (e.g., corporation, partnership, or sole proprietorship); (3) Your share of the business; (4) Your position in the business; (5) Other owners, their shares and relationship to you; (6) Whether there is a buy/sell agreement; and (7) Desired disposition of your share.

(Note: This is an opportunity to discuss the business, its succession and its value in the context of estate planning so that a spouse who is not the business owner can get a realistic handle on what the value of the business is and what can be expected in the event of the owner's death.)

Your Estimate of Value of the Business

	$		$

g. Miscellaneous:

(i.e., expected inheritances; valuable personal property; promissory notes payable to you; any other special factors which may affect your situation).

 (Note: This is designed to highlight when the plan may have to be changed or revised. If, for example, if you are expecting an additional inheritance when you parents or grandparents die, then the plan may have to be completely revamped at that time.)

_____

_____

_____

_____

h. Prior Gifts:

(Itemize significant past gifts [over $13,000/yr.] to any one individual made by you; indicate whether you filed gift tax returns.)

(Note: This is important to keep track of, because once you go past the $13,000 per year annual exclusion then - with the exceptions of making a gift for anyone's medical or educational expenses and making such payments directly to the provider - you are making a taxable gift. Also, once you go through your federal lifetime gifting allotment (currently $5,000,000 for each of you), you reduce the amount that could pass tax free at your death.)

_____

_____

_____

_____

i. Assets of Minor Children

If you have any minor children state whether any such child has separate assets (such as custodial accounts), including approximate amounts and in whose name they are held:

(Note: This information will enable your estate planner to determine whether the sums are enough for future tuition, on one hand, and, on the other hand, and if the accounts in the children's names might be "overfunded" – whether the children will have too much money to do with as they please when they reach the age of 21.)

_____

_____

_____

_____

IV. Liabilities

Indicate significant debts and debts guaranteed by you [excluding mortgages listed earlier], as well as lawsuits, or claims, present or anticipated.

(Note: If there are significant mortgages or personal guarantees, it is important to know which member of the couple is obligated on them, and whether a life insurance policy needs to be put in place to cover those liabilities if personal assets are at risk. Sometimes the commercial financing institutions will mandate that these liabilities be covered by life insurance.)

_____

_____

_____

Total Liabilities

	$		$	Joint with others	$

V. Financial Recap

Please list the total values from Items III A to G:

(Note: Putting a financial recap together and discussing it is very important and should be done on a regular basis. Knowing how assets are titled – whose name is on what – raises key estate planning issues. In many states, for example, if an asset is titled by joint owner-ship with a right of survivorship it will pass to the surviving joint owner regardless of what your will says. It is important also to highlight assets here that are owned jointly with oth-ers – and property that is owned as tenants in common without a survivorship right.)

			JOINT/TRUST
Real Estate	$	$	$
Bank Assets	$	$	$
Stocks, etc.	$	$	$
Retirement	$	$	$
Insurance	$	$	$
Business	$	$	$
Miscellaneous	$	$	$
Totals	$	$	$
Liabilities (Including Mortgages)	$ ( )	$ ( )	$ ( )
Net Assets	$	$	$

VI: Planning Issues

a. Your Goals:

Please briefly state your estate planning goals (e.g. tax minimization, financial well-being and education of children, protection of business, charitable goals, etc.):

_____

b. Long Term Care Insurance

Long term care insurance, either standing alone or in conjunction with Medicaid planning, can help prevent the depletion of your assets if you should ever require nursing home or other long term care, including care in your home.

Are you currently covered by a long term care insurance policy? _____

If so, please submit a copy of your policy and any explanatory or descriptive literature you may have received.

If you are not covered, would you like to discuss long term care insurance?

c. Disability Insurance

Are you covered by a disability insurance policy? _____

If yes: Amount of coverage _____

Waiting period _____

Duration of benefit _____

If you are not covered, would you like to discuss disability insurance coverage? _____

VII. Disposition of Assets: Explain in a general way how you wish to dispose of your property (desired shares for children, relatives, charity, etc.)

(Note: Thinking through these issues ahead of time – how much you wish your children, nieces, nephews, other relatives to receive, who is to be primary beneficiary, who needs special protection – will highlight any areas of disagreement and make a discussion to iron out the differences more productive.)

_____

_____

_____

_____

_____

VIII. Fiduciaries

Whom are you considering as possible candidates to serve as your Executor or Trustee, and Guardian of your minor children?

(Note: In most instances you will be the initial trustee (s) of the respective trusts; you must think about the selection of a successor. Giving some thought to the fiduciary decision in advance of the initial meeting – even if you are not really sure – provides a jump start to the discussion. In the guardian arena, for example, it forces you to put down a name. For many people this is a stumbling block. Give some thought to this on your own and we will discuss it at the meeting.)

Executor(s)		Address	
Successor Executor(s)		Address	
Guardian(s)		Address	
Successor Guardian(s)		Address	
Trustee(s)		Address	
Successor Trustee(s)		Address	

IX. Your Professional Advisors

(Note: It is a good idea to have a comprehensive list of all advisors that your executor or successor trustee would be able to locate if you become disabled or at your death. In many circumstances, such as when there is a family business involved, it helps to have the advisors to meet as a team – annually or more frequently. Having the entire team together in dialogue can lead to open discussions and a better result.)

Accountant		Telephone	
Attorney		Telephone	
Insurance Advisor		Telephone	
Financial Planner		Telephone	
Stockbroker		Telephone	

X. Safe Deposit

Safe deposit box location and persons having access:

_____

XI. Additional Comments/Questions Include below any additional comments, concerns, information, or specific questions you wish to have answered in the estate planning process:

_____

_____

_____

_____

_____

XII. Please attach photocopies of the following documents: Attached (X) or N/A

Wills and codicils, if any: _____

Trust Instruments in which you have an interest: _____

Deeds to Real Estate: _____

Most, recent Federal and State Income Tax Returns: _____

All Gift Tax Returns: _____

Pre or Post Nuptial Agreements: _____

Separation Agreements, Divorce Papers: _____

Life Insurance Policies: _____

Business Agreements and Documents
regarding Interests in Closely Held Business: _____

Retirement Plans or Other Information from
Plan Administrator: _____

7936151R0

Made in the USA
Charleston, SC
23 April 2011